LET
THIS
MIND
BE IN
YOU

LET THIS MIND BE IN YOU

Exploring
God's Call to
Servanthood

James K. Dew Jr.

PUBLISHING
BRENTWOOD, TENNESSEE

978-1-0877-8871-5

Published by B&H Publishing Group
Brentwood, Tennessee

Dewey Decimal Classification: 253.7
Subject Heading: SERVANTHOOD, CHRISTIAN \
CLERGY \ MINISTRY

Cover design by B&H Publishing Group.
Brain wire frame model by Jezper/Alamy.
Author photo by NOBTS staff.

1 2 3 4 5 6 • 27 26 25 24 23

To Tara:

The sweetest servant I know

Acknowledgments

This is not the kind of book I ever expected to write, but I am thankful for the opportunity to do so. Over the past few years, the Lord has been incredibly kind to me, bringing conviction and correction from seasons of pride and burdening my heart to offer myself as a servant. This book represents all that I aspire to be in Christ, and it has been good for my soul to put it on paper.

When discussion with my friends at B&H started several months ago, I knew exactly what I wanted to write about, so I'd like to thank them for offering me this opportunity. Specifically, I'd like to thank Devin Maddox for planting the seed in my mind and encouraging me to take up this task. I'd also like to thank Madison Trammel for being a fantastic editor. Both of these men offered helpful feedback as my ideas began to formulate.

I'd also like to thank a large group of folks at New Orleans Baptist Theological Seminary for the past few years of dialogue about servanthood. What started as a burden in my heart has been cultivated through our conversations and shared work in training the next generation of servants.

To our students, you are exactly the kind of people I want to spend my life serving. You bought into our vision for servanthood and came to campus to learn with us what it means. I love that about you. You give me hope for who we can be as Southern Baptists. At so many points along the way as I wrote these chapters, I thought of you, seeing in my mind the many ways I've observed you embodying the kind of servanthood I describe in these pages. Thank you for being who you are and for joining us in our quest to be the servants God calls us to be. May we continue striving together to be servants who walk with Christ, proclaim His truth, and fulfill His mission.

Thanks also to my administrative team and faculty for buying into the calling of servanthood. I came to New Orleans with a yearning for servanthood, only to find that the faculty and administration of our great school were already marked by it. You've been an inspiration and encouragement to me in ways I'll never be able to convey. I'm proud to have you as my friends and colaborers in this work. Thanks especially to my cabinet—Norris Grubbs, Larry Lyon, Thomas Strong, Mike Wetzel, Bo Rice, Greg Wilton, Laurie Watts, and Chris Shaffer—for our many conversations on servanthood and for leading with me in this. To Bo Rice, Chris Shaffer, and Norris

Grubbs, thank you for driving as I hammered out chapters on our various trips. Special thanks also to Chris Shaffer, Jordan Faison, and my wife, Tara, for reading every chapter of this book in such short order. You all are the best. I am grateful for each of you.

Finally, and most importantly, thank you to my wonderful wife, Tara, and our four incredible children—Natalie, Nathan, Samantha, and Samuel. My goodness, I love you guys! Thanks not only for letting me do the things I do but also for stepping into it with me and making everything better by your presence. The work we do is not just my ministry; it is our ministry, and I am so proud of each of you. Please know that Daddy loves you and you're more important to me than anything this side of heaven.

Contents

Foreword

Servanthood—the character that causes us to place others before ourselves, helping where people have need, and finding joy in a life that is focused on others." That definition of servanthood, proposed by Jamie Dew, confronts both contemporary evangelical culture and the prideful heart of every human being.

Evangelical Christianity is best known for its celebrities, the men and women who have risen to national and global notoriety through their writings, broadcasts, and conferences. Far too often, these celebrities' personal lives are marked by opulent wealth derived from their "ministry," moral inconsistencies at odds with their teachings, or arrogant attitudes that enable them to treat with contempt the individuals and institutions responsible for providing their platforms and fostering their fame. While some publicly feign humility, too few manage to maintain that posture in private.

From where does this failure of Christian leaders to model the servant's heart of our Savior come? As the old cliché reminds us, the heart of the matter is the matter of the heart.

Celebrity Christians are not, of course, the only ones who struggle with the prideful nature of the human heart. This heart condition is universal to every human being. Sin, at its root, is always traceable to a heart of pride, a heart in love with itself, protecting itself, pleasuring itself, and placing itself above others. Putting pen and paper to the list of my own sins, I have found that the ink of each is always the color of pride.

In contrast, Jesus embodied servanthood and called his disciples to follow his example because servanthood is the tangible exhibition of a humbled heart. I intentionally use the word 'humbled' rather than 'humble.' The human heart is never humble until or unless it has been humbled. Any ounce of humility that might be observable in my life, and those combined ounces would not fill a teacup, resulted almost exclusively from humiliation. The human heart is marked by the Fall and the same sin that led to the fall, the sin of human pride, inhabits every heart, since every heart bears the curse of Adam. But God, by His grace, often orchestrates the circumstances of our lives in humiliating ways, ways that foster humility. The pathway to humility preferred by our Savior, however, is that of humiliating ourselves by assuming the role of a servant.

In teaching this truth to his disciples, Jesus recognized the risks. Chief among those risks is that the one who serves would consider himself to have achieved greatness, and thus ironically again fallen victim to his prideful heart. So, Jesus, in what I consider one of the most helpful lessons on the topic of pride, references what a master still expects of a servant who has come in from the fields. Using that scenario, Jesus states, "So you also, when you have done all that you were commanded, say, 'We are unworthy servants; we have only done what was our duty'" (Luke 17:10).

For humility's sake, Jesus not only calls his disciples to be servants but, in being servants, to constantly humble themselves.

I know Jamie Dew well enough to know he would never author a book on humility. Such an endeavor would suggest that he had mastered the topic, or at least that he was running far enough ahead of the rest of us that he could teach us a thing or two about being humble. I've observed enough humility in Jamie's life and heard the testimony of how God has humiliated him for his own good, to know he would never make that arrogant assumption. Instead, Jamie has given us the gift of shining the spotlight on Scripture's pathway to humility, i.e., servanthood.

Jamie will remark in the introduction that this book is a departure from his usual subject matter. His other books, he points out, are philosophical or apologetic in nature. "For my entire career," he observes, "I have been concerned with the 'big questions' related to our faith and have given myself to their pursuit, working hard to help my students think well about their faith."

Having been given by the author the privilege of writing this preface to his book, the reader may be surprised that I would take this opportunity to engage in a debate with the author of the very book I'm commending to you. Nevertheless, I must cite two critical points of disagreement with the author. First, I do not believe that Jamie Dew has departed from his usual subject matter. Rather, I believe he has deepened his—and our—understanding of that subject matter. The most convincing proof of the truth of Christian philosophy, a biblical worldview, or Christian apologetics, is the genuine servant of Christ and others.

Second, in engaging the biblical nature of servanthood, Dew has not departed from "the 'big questions' related to our faith" nor failed to help "students think well about their faith." Rather, he has arrived at the biggest question of faith and helped students think well about the most important aspect of faith. The earliest confession of the Church was, "Jesus is Lord." What does that confession entail and require of those who make it if not the call to serve the Lord Jesus? And what does it mean to serve Jesus? In the pages of this book, you will find the apologetic.

Paul Chitwood
President of the International Mission Board of the SBC

Introduction

L et *This Mind Be in You* is a book about servanthood in the life of Christians in ministry. Taken from Philippians 2:5, the title captures the call that is placed on our lives as followers of Jesus Christ, especially those who are called into His ministry. In the pages that follow, we will explore God's call to approach our ministries with a posture and disposition that is pleasing to the Lord, life-giving for us, and helpful to the people we serve. I firmly believe servanthood is essential to every form of Christian service, and it is impossible to please God with any other posture. As servants, we joyfully flourish when we take up this disposition. But what exactly is servanthood? As a working definition, let's think of it this way:

> *Servanthood*—the character trait that causes us to place others before ourselves, helping where people have need and finding joy in a life that is focused on others.

At first glance, it may seem unnecessary to say we must adopt the posture of servants. *After all,* we might think, *we are ministers of the gospel. Of course we are servant oriented! Isn't servanthood a given among those who are ministers?* In short, no, it is not. Not at all. Most of us noticed after just a short time in ministry, by paying attention to our own lives or by watching the lives of others, that what we are supposed to be is not always what we are. Because of spotlights, platforms, frustrations, hardships, successes, failures, applause, criticism, and many other aspects of ministry, we can become as self-focused, self-absorbed, attention seeking, glory grabbing, and boastful as anyone on the planet. Pride can take root in us and dominate us just as it can anyone else. Selfish ambition can overwhelm our plans. We can become addicted to attention. But this is not the way it is supposed to be.

Jesus Christ was a servant, and He called us to follow Him by doing what He did. The posture and lifestyle of a servant runs in the opposite direction from our natural instincts and appetites. Servanthood must be intentionally sought and diligently cultivated. In some small measure, I hope to model that cultivation in the pages that follow.

A Quick Confession and Prayer

This is not the kind of book I normally write or contribute to, as all my writing up to this point has been philosophical or apologetic. Throughout my career, I have been concerned with the "big questions" related to our faith and have given myself to their pursuit, working hard to help my students think well about their faith. I still love that kind of work and look forward to doing more of it in years to come. Recently, however, I have become increasingly concerned with spiritual formation. It's not that I didn't care about it before. But the older I get, the more I see how central it is and what has been life-giving in my ministry and what has not.

God has been incredibly kind to me, gently reminding me these past few years where my greatest joy is found. As a child whose parents split up when I was seven, who failed two grades, was arrested a few times in high school, and graduated with a 1.6 GPA, I never assumed my life could be used for anything of kingdom value. But after twenty-eight years of grace, I've been blessed to pastor, teach at the seminary level, and serve as the president of New Orleans Baptist Theological Seminary. As God transformed my life, He brought opportunities for responsibility, influence, titles, and positions of honor. In each of those opportunities, I discovered there were also chances to chase fame, seek attention, jockey for position, and make much of my feeble accomplishments.

Yet titles, influence, and recognition never satisfied my soul the way Christ Himself first did long ago. As I look back across these past twenty-eight years of being a Christian, the moments that were most life-giving and fruitful didn't come when I sat at the highest levels or enjoyed the greatest recognition. Instead, the richest, most satisfying seasons of my life have been those where the primary care of my heart was to know Christ and make Him known. More specifically, the most wonderful seasons of my life have been those when Christ was my greatest treasure and serving Him was my greatest aspiration.

As I write this book, I serve as president of one of the largest theological institutions of the evangelical world, New Orleans Baptist Theological Seminary. But I hold this responsibility mindful that I can never please my Lord without the posture and disposition of a servant. I write this book, therefore, not as one who has already become the servant I'm supposed to be but as one who desperately wants to please my Lord and to discern what a life of servanthood looks like. I welcome you to join me in this journey. May the Lord grant us the favor to become the servants He created us to be as we take these steps together.

What Will We Cover?

Part 1 consists of two chapters. In them, I take an honest look at some real problems before turning to the call of servanthood in the book's next two parts. Chapter 1 surveys the world and all its brokenness. Our world has plenty of problems, but the biggest is that it is filled with greedy, prideful, and self-centered people. The results of this are always pain and sorrow. The world longs to see something different in us, but unfortunately, even those of us who are called to be servants can become just as prideful and self-centered as anyone else. Chapter 2 explores the problem of pride in the Christian minister's heart. Here I take an unflinching look at the causes of pride and arrogance in the minister's life. In the interest of self-promotion and self-glorification, we can worship at the idol of our own name, seeking platforms, spotlights, and the applause of our peers. All of this is contrary to the call on our lives as Christ followers. We must be honest about these appetites and influences so they can be destroyed and avoided.

Part 2, consisting of chapters 3 through 5, begins an exploration into servanthood that occupies the remainder of the book. Against the backdrop of our prideful appetites, chapter 3 investigates anew the call to servanthood presented in both Old and New Testaments. I note what God has to say about servanthood in the law, the prophets, the Psalms and Proverbs, and the apostles' letters. I also offer at least five distinct virtues that servants of the Lord should possess— humility, obedience, sacrifice, trust, and devotion. In chapter 4, I turn our focus to Jesus, the perfect embodiment of those virtues and, because of this, our example to follow. Chapter 5 then explores what it means to be a servant. I examine what a virtue is and demonstrate the impact virtues have on both individuals and on those around them.

In part 3, chapter 6 considers what satisfies the heart of a servant. I contend that a servant can only give his whole life by finding great joy in Jesus, but that once he has found this joy, he will lay everything down to serve Him. Chapter 6 argues that the posture of servanthood is impossible until we find our primary satisfaction in Christ. Only when our hearts are set on Him, when our affections for Him are regularly cultivated, will we become the servants God calls us to be. Chapter 7 demonstrates that while servanthood manifests itself in virtually every action, Christian servants are diligent to couple their service with clear gospel proclamation. Whether teaching, preaching, or sharing through friendships, true servants tell others about Jesus. Expanding on the themes of chapter 7, chapter 8 focuses on the servant's responsibility to the nations. In the same way the Son of God left His throne and came to those who walk in darkness, His servants take the gospel to people who remain in darkness. As the global population continues to skyrocket, those who serve Jesus must redouble their efforts to fulfill the Great Commission.

Finally, chapter 9 offers a focused examination of Philippians 2:1–11, the passage from which this book gets its title. As profound as this great Christological portion of

Philippians is theologically, the apostle Paul offers it to us as an illustration of the servanthood we are called to in 2:2–5. Having charged us to "do nothing out of selfish ambition or conceit" and to "let each of you look out not only for [your] own interests, but also for the interest of others" (NKJV), we are then told to "let this mind be in you which was also in Christ Jesus" (NKJV). The divine Son took the posture of a servant; thus, we are called to do the same.

Jesus Christ came into this world to serve broken people who were lost in their sin, and He calls us to follow Him in that service. I look forward to exploring what this means more fully in the chapters to come. I'm praying for you as you aspire to servanthood with me.

Part 1

Why Do We Need to Think about Servanthood?

Why do we need to think about servanthood? The first two chapters of this book are an attempt to answer this question. Most of the book will be spent focusing on what servants are (part 2—chapters 3–5) and what servants do (part 3—chapters 6–9). It will also attempt to cast a compelling vision for who we are supposed to be as followers of Jesus Christ. But before we can do those things, we must first understand why servanthood is needed today and why we, as ministers of the gospel, need to give our attention to this important calling.

These first two chapters are hard hitting. In them we pull the cover back and take an honest look at what is wrong with our world and what unfortunately happens to so many ministers of the gospel. The world is filled with greed, pride, and selfishness, and it is terribly broken as a result. As servants of the Lord, we are called to enter into this brokenness. This calling requires humility, compassion, and servanthood in those that do the work of ministry. But ironically, as we will discuss in detail in chapter 2, ministry has a unique way of feeding our pride and causing us to become egocentric. When this happens, we become everything we are not supposed to be.

It's not always pleasant to dwell on the bad news about our world and about us as ministers. But if we are going to talk about servanthood for the rest of the book, we may as well be honest at the beginning of our journey about the problems that afflict us.

Chapter 1

A World without Servants

C hrist was a servant, and He calls us, His followers, to be servants with Him. We will explore this in greater depth in the chapters that follow, chapters 3 through 9 specifically. But before we explore that call to servanthood, it is important to set the context for why such servanthood is essential. It is important for us to get a clear picture of the world we live in and just how broken it is and also to be honest about the way our egos and pride cause those of us in ministry to miss this calling of servanthood. The world is filled with darkness, and we are called, as servants of Jesus Christ, to take His light into that darkness. So we will explore God's call on our lives, but we must first understand the context into which we are called.

The world is not as it ought to be. Everywhere we look, we see people hurting, families being ripped apart, and lives destroyed by sin. This has always been true, but it's particularly true right now. The past few decades have conditioned us to be as hostile toward one another as possible. But events of the past three years have intensified things to the point that turmoil surrounds us everywhere we look. Civility is dead, and its lack is destroying much of our culture. The advent of social media has only exacerbated the issue. Where there is trouble, social media is an unending supply of fuel to the fires of controversy. The divisions among us are many, and almost every issue we face is polarizing. We find this to be true in our families, our political institutions, our schools, and even our churches and denominations.

Many of the problems we face are rooted in the basic disposition to be selfish, prideful, and greedy. When these appetites reign in us, they choke out everything that is life-giving and helpful to people, both individually and collectively. When we only care about ourselves, it is a perfect recipe for destruction. Even more problematic, it's displeasing to God and contrary to what we are called to be.

A Greedy, Prideful, and Self-Centered World

Why exactly are things so broken? We described the hostility of our world in the paragraphs above, but we should want to know why it is this way. To be sure, there are a lot of problems in our world, and there are multiple contributors. I don't want to offer a reductionistic account of our problems that oversimplifies the situation or ignores complexities. But I do want to suggest that, complex variables aside, most of our problems really are heart problems rooted in greed, pride, and self-centeredness.

We tend to think of these sinful dispositions as "minor" sins, having no massive impact on people around us. We think these sins reside only in us and never actually hurt other people. Because of this, we think these sinful dispositions are less problematic than the "big sins" of rape, murder, incest, and adultery. But that perspective is naïve and has to be incorrect. It's naïve because it fails to understand that God sees all sin as evil. It's naïve because it assumes that the so-called "bigger" social sins of rape, murder, and the like aren't rooted in the dispositions of greed, pride, and self-centeredness. Underneath all of those horrific actions are the same sinful dispositions of greed, pride, and self-centeredness. People do terrible things because they disregard other people around them. Sure, there are probably other factors that brought them to the place of committing terrible acts, but whatever those other factors may be, they are added to and draped upon a disposition that cares more for self than for others. Horrible acts may be more than just evil dispositions, but they are not less.

Consider the way greed impacts people's lives. Greed is an appetite and disposition that craves more, even when enough is already owned. The greedy person will reach for things he shouldn't reach for, while hurting other people in the process. This leads to actions of dishonesty, theft, and manipulation that end in sorrow and trauma. The greedy person will walk over people to get what he wants because he is consumed with his own desires. As such, greedy people are hurtful people. Proverbs 28:25 says, "A greedy person stirs up conflict, but whoever trusts in the LORD will prosper." We see examples of this verse all around us. People, businesses, scammers, family members, and even religious people con others out of what is rightfully theirs, leaving destruction in their path.

Or consider the way pride wounds people. Pride is a disposition that causes us either to think more highly of ourselves than we should, to place ourselves at the center of everything, or both. Prideful people are always right about things, at least in their own minds. Prideful people disregard the feelings, thoughts, ideas, and needs of everyone around them because they are so fixated on themselves. As the Bible tells us, "Pride comes before destruction, and an arrogant spirit before a fall" (Prov. 16:18). Those who are consumed by pride hurt other people around them simply by not caring about them. But pride can also cause us to hurt people more directly. When pride rules in our hearts, we become rude and critical, inflicting damage on people we should otherwise care for and support.

Both greed and pride are versions of selfishness and self-centeredness. Our most natural thought in most cases is about ourselves. We put ourselves before other people, insisting that we be cared for first, leaving the leftovers for the people around us. When we do this, we forsake God's blessings on our lives. According to Proverbs 11:25, "A generous person will be enriched, and the one who gives a drink of water will receive water." And Proverbs 21:13 says, "The one who shuts his ears to the cry of the poor will himself also call out and not be answered." There is no life in selfishness. We miss what God has for us, and we miss the opportunity to care for others who need our help.

When people are consumed with greed, pride, and selfishness, bad results must come. It simply isn't true that people controlled by these things "aren't hurting anybody else." There may be moments when they are not actively hurting other people, but they will absolutely cause harm and pain to others. And it may be true that there is more going on in a bad situation than a person's selfishness and pride, yet selfishness and pride can clearly be at play. When they are present, problems will surely come as a result. Like a disease that kills a body, these sins kill and destroy the person who tolerates them and the people they impact.

Desperate for Something Different

Such is the world we live in. We see these dispositions in every aspect of our culture—in sports, politics, families, and schools. The resulting hostility generates fatigue and stress. Because of this, many people long to see, experience, and be a part of something different. Our world longs for people who are not characterized by greed, pride, and selfishness, people who are helpful and caring, people who are loving. Our world is desperate to find these people, but they are hard to locate. Our calling to love and care for others is the antidote to the sicknesses in our world. We are called to abandon our greed, pride, and selfishness and take the posture of a servant and love the people God puts before us. Our calling is to be the people our broken world longs to encounter.

What would such people be like? For starters, they would be a people who are focused on following Jesus. In chapter 8, I will say much more about this, but for now let me simply say we need to think literally about what it means to be a follower of Jesus. A follower goes where He goes, does what He does, loves what He loves, and is about what He is about. We confess this to be true but tend to think of following Jesus in mere theological terms. That is, we think that as long as we articulate our doctrine correctly, that is what matters most. A follower will in fact be diligent to affirm the teachings of

Christ and Scripture. Still, following requires much more. We must follow Him in both word and deed. If our words are correct but our dispositions and attitudes are wrong, we aren't actually following Him. Because of this, the servant this world longs for is one who follows Christ in what he affirms but also in the way he interacts with people. These servants are selfless, thinking less of themselves than they do of others, willingly placing others' needs before their own.

Moreover, a true servant of the Lord will be a person who is characterized by a particular set of virtues—namely, humility, obedience, sacrifice, trust, and devotion. I will say much about this in chapter 5, but for now I will simply note that servanthood is about being a particular kind of person, a person who has a certain kind of character. The world does not often encounter such people, but when they do, they immediately recognize that something is different. They long to meet people who are humble, obedient, sacrificial, trusting, and devout—the virtues Christian servants possess.

Servants of Christ also learn to crucify the idols of fame, power, and money. We will look at the desires for these things in the next chapter. Ministers of the gospel are called to be servants. Ironically enough, in ministry we often become all the things we aren't supposed to be. Ministry hits us with a unique mix of experiences that cause us to crave attention and seek the spotlight. All of this is antithetical to who Christ is, and it is also antithetical to who we are called to be as His followers. Our idols of greed, pride, and selfishness cause us to be less like Him, but that doesn't mean we have to remain that way. As we recognize these idols and turn from them, we grow in humility and begin to resemble Him. As we pursue servanthood, we posture ourselves humbly before others, pursuing the good of the people around us.

Moving Forward

In chapters 3 through 9, we explore God's call on us to be servants and what this means for the way we live our lives. God's call is both beautiful and life-giving. It causes us to place others first, helping where they have need and finding joy in a life that is focused on them. Before we delve into servanthood more deeply, we need first to take an honest look at the way we, as ministers of the gospel, often become something we shouldn't.

Chapter 2

Platforms, Applause, and the Idol of Our Own Name

Nearly everyone enjoys attention. Some of us, however, crave it in the deepest levels of our being. More specifically, we crave positive attention. We like a word of encouragement, a kind affirmation, or a compliment on how we have handled something. For many of us, positive attention determines the way we interact with other people and even the things we pursue. I first noticed this as a child in elementary school. I noticed how much better I liked my life when others thought well of me and how poorly I felt about life when they didn't. I also noticed it in my classmates. I noticed it in the way little boys bragged about their athletic ability, little girls relished in their popularity, and some kids gravitated toward the spotlight. Some kids, for example, were so gifted that school just seemed natural to them, both academically and socially. The teachers loved them, and they embraced the role of being the teacher's best students. In all the various ways it manifested itself, even as a young kid, I noticed quickly that there was something inside all of us that instinctively seeks attention.

This craving is so instinctual that, interestingly, some people will take attention any way they can get it, even if it is negative in nature. For instance, I vividly recall a fellow student who seemed incapable of achieving positive attention from our teachers. He seemed to create trouble simply so he could have the attention of the teacher in some way each day. This student struggled with his grades, wasn't particularly popular, and never received a word of praise for the way he conducted himself in our class. I didn't know much about his home life, but from what I did know, it wasn't good. His father was rarely home, and his family was relatively poor. His home life was tough, and one couldn't help but feel bad for him. Every day he talked out of turn, poked a classmate in the eye, stole another kid's snack at recess, or bullied other kids on the playground—all so the teacher would pay attention to him.

This drive for attention is rooted in something more primitive. We are communal in nature, we have a deep need to belong, and we desire to be loved by other people. These cravings are instinctual, as we are made by God to belong to Him and to others. But these cravings can manifest themselves in our lives through the inappropriate pursuit of attention.

Thankfully, God Himself is the answer to our cravings. He made us for Himself, and the belonging we seek is resolved in communion with Him. King David understood this well; in Psalm 23 he said, "The LORD is my shepherd; I have what I need." In other words, because David had God, he had everything that he both needed and wanted. He was satisfied. Saint Augustine famously acknowledged the same thought in the opening prayer of his work *Confessions*: "You made us for yourself and our hearts find no peace until they rest in you."[1] For Augustine, God Himself—not a doctrine, not a calling, not a title or position, and certainly not the attention or praise of other people—brought satisfaction to his greatest longings.

Ministry and the Craving for Attention

In the best version of ourselves, we are servants: humble, kind, unassuming, and eager to serve God and people. In the worst version of ourselves, however, we are like the peacock. None of us intend to become peacocks, at least I pray we don't. But ministry has the ability, if we aren't careful, to bring out the peacock in all of us.

The peacock is a midsize bird that is adorned with feathers which make him appear much bigger and more impressive than he actually is. This bird will stretch his feathers out as wide as possible, strut in front of other animals, and pretend to be large and intimidating. I've learned over years of ministry that some preachers and ministers do the same thing. They name-drop, mention the big events where they speak, and strut around with their entourage. They seem more impressive than they actually are.

We tend to lose sight of the fact that our greatest joy is found in humble obedience to Jesus. And we somehow come to think that worldly spotlights and platforms will make us happy and fulfilled. Let me be honest. I've seen this happen in many people over the years, but I have seen this behavior most often in myself. God forgive us. None of us intended to become peacocks, yet sometimes we do. It is the opposite of what we are called to be, and it cannot possibly satisfy our souls; only humble obedience to Christ will lead us to satisfaction. Somehow, some way, we must kill that peacock inside us all.

We know God alone can satisfy the greatest longings of our souls. We hear this over and over in church, and we even preach this truth regularly to other people. Yet aspects of our ministries cause us to ignore this truth and live as if it weren't true. Functionally, we reject the truth by seeking our satisfaction in things—like platforms, applause, and fame— that will only leave us dissatisfied and less like Christ.

Life in ministry is unique and multifaceted, and the people who give themselves to this life are as well. Ministers of the gospel answer God's call to Christian service and in many cases leave behind career opportunities, significant money, and comfortable lives of leisure so they can serve Christ and His people. In one sense, they are selfless people who put God and others before themselves. Or, at least, most ministers start off that way. But as we all learn quickly, the wrong circumstances, coupled with a lack of spiritual diligence, can lead ministers of the gospel to become as prideful, self-centered, and glory seeking as anyone on the planet. Let's consider three factors that bring about this change.

Natural Desire for Affirmation

I've already mentioned this point above, so I will be brief. Since God made us to be communal beings, it is natural to want to be accepted by the people we love and to know that who we are and what we do are worth something. Yet this natural desire can become corrupted quickly, so that we are consumed by a need for approval, attention, and affirmation. Once we add the unique circumstances of ministry to the mix, along with a lack of spiritual discipline, we will be heading in a dangerously wrong direction.

Toxic Circumstances

Ministry often thrusts us into a unique set of circumstances that, if left unaddressed, will be a perfect storm for our pride and ego. The rhythms and routines of ministry expose some of our greatest insecurities and feed our worst appetites. On the one hand, pastors and ministers are often the focal point of criticisms and complaints. Church members criticize the pastor's preaching, how seldom he visits the sick, how much money he makes, who his friends are, the imperfections in his wife and children, the lack of growth in the church, and so much more. For many in ministry, no matter what they do or how much they give, they are the constant focus of criticism. In addition to this, church members often resist the pastor's leadership, especially if it requires any form of change. As a result, discouragement and frustration can dominate our minds on many days, causing us to envy every other pastor who appears to serve in far greener pastures. These realities create dispositions and desires in us that will, if left to themselves, grow into destructive qualities.

However, the criticisms we receive and frustrations we face are only half of the toxic circumstances we confront. Pastors and ministers are also the focal point of affirmation, attention, and praise. While one group of people criticize us constantly, another group lavishes praise on us, affirming every decision we make, every message we preach, and everything we accomplish. In addition, we are constantly on platforms, given kind introductions before we speak, and celebrated by those who love us. These experiences may seem to contradict those in the previous paragraph, but they don't. Both sides of the coin are true, and together they create the perfect storm for our egos to grow and consume us.

The frustrations and envy created in us by criticism from one group lead to a craving for affirmation and appreciation. As that craving takes root, we begin to obsess over the attention and appreciation given to us by another group. In short, the strange ministry combination of criticism and affirmation creates a toxic set of circumstances that we must be vigilant to protect our hearts against. Unfortunately, our responses to these realities are often too little, too late.

Lack of Spiritual Discipline

Coupled with the natural desire for affirmation and the toxic circumstances created by criticism and praise, we often lack the spiritual discipline to keep our hearts in check. I've been in theological education and around ministers of the gospel for the past twenty-four years. In that time, I have seen a familiar pattern take shape in far too many of us. When we come to faith in Jesus, we are broken by our sin and feel ourselves desperate for Him in every way. When we first encounter His grace, our love and affection for Him overflow. We read the Bible with curiosity and eagerness, and we find joy in each nugget of God's truth we discover. We have a lot of sin to overcome, but we are diligent to repent and seek His grace in every part of our lives. Like little children, we look to our Lord to provide for us and keep us near Himself.

Over time we begin to change. What started as a deeply personal and spiritual enterprise morphs into something different. We study and prepare for ministry, giving careful attention to our theology, hermeneutics, and exegesis. We grow in our speaking abilities and in the process become professional communicators. We develop leadership skills by navigating difficult situations. Let me be clear—these are all good things. Yet what started out as a deeply personal and spiritual enterprise becomes academic and professional. In the process, we forget where our joy, power, and wisdom are found. Our prayer life wanes, and we seldom read the Bible for purposes outside sermon preparation. We become slow to repent, and patterns of sin take root in our lives. All the spiritual disciplines begin to diminish. When this becomes true of us, we are in the most vulnerable position we could be in, ripe for all the wrong forces to shape us.

So here we are, a people who end up forsaking the servanthood we were called to, consumed by a deep desire to be known and esteemed. As I noted at the beginning of this chapter, like all other people in the world, by virtue of being human, we have an instinctual desire for attention and affirmation. As we settle into the rhythms of ministry, we encounter a toxic mixture of criticism and praise that encourages all the wrong dispositions in our minds and hearts. This context, along with the lack of spiritual discipline to guard our attitudes and cultivate Christian virtues, causes us to become what we aren't supposed to be.

Before we know it, and often without realizing it, we lose sight of the servants we are called to be and have become consumed with aspiration for platforms, applause, and bigger churches or ministry assignments. We didn't start off this way, and we never meant for it to happen, but we have become self-consumed, serving the idol of our own name. We want others to make much of us. We want to be celebrated. We want people to know what a big deal we are. In the end we just want fame and greatness. All of this is the opposite of who Jesus Christ is and whom He called us to be.

The Debate for Greatness and Jesus's Call to Humility and Servanthood

We are not alone in this poor state. Jesus's disciples were often controlled by the same desires. All three Synoptic Gospel writers report the disciples' debate over who was the greatest among them. In Matthew 18:1–4; Mark 9:33–37; and Luke

9:46–48, we find that they were plagued by the same sinful dispositions that afflict us. Significantly, we find one of the most important instructions for our souls in Jesus's response to them. Mark's account (9:33–37) includes the most detail. It says:

> They came to Capernaum. When he was in the house, he asked them, "What were you arguing about on the way?" But they were silent, because on the way they had been arguing with one another about who was the greatest. Sitting down, he called the Twelve and said to them, "If anyone wants to be first, he must be last and servant of all." He took a child, had him stand among them, and taking him in his arms, he said to them, "Whoever welcomes one little child such as this in my name welcomes me. And whoever welcomes me does not welcome me, but him who sent me."

We read these stories and are shocked by the selfish candor of the disciples. In the passage just before these verses (9:30–32), Jesus warned them of His coming death and resurrection. Yet they didn't seem to care about that or to consider what God might be wanting to do through them. Instead they focused on their own greatness.

In response Jesus told them that true greatness is the opposite of what the world thinks. Greatness is not found in high positions or stature. Rather it is found in those who become servants to all. "If anyone wants to be first," Jesus said, "he must be last and servant of all" (Mark 9:35). He put a child before them as an example of the humility He seeks. Matthew 18:3–4 adds that "unless you turn and become like little children, you will never enter the kingdom of heaven. Therefore, whoever humbles himself like this child—this one is the greatest in the kingdom of heaven." Greatness, Jesus told us, is found in humility and servanthood.

What is particularly troubling about the disciples in this story, however, is that they still didn't seem to understand what Jesus had just warned them about. Having just been rebuked by Jesus in Mark 9 (see also Matt. 18 and Luke 9), the disciples remained consumed by the same aspiration for greatness in the next chapter (Mark 10:35–45).

> James and John, the sons of Zebedee, approached him and said, "Teacher, we want you to do whatever we ask you."
>
> "What do you want me to do for you?" he asked them.
>
> They answered him, "Allow us to sit at your right and at your left in your glory."

Jesus said to them, "You don't know what you're asking. Are you able to drink the cup I drink or to be baptized with the baptism I am baptized with?"

"We are able," they told him.

Jesus said to them, "You will drink the cup I drink, and you will be baptized with the baptism I am baptized with. But to sit at my right or left is not mine to give; instead, it is for those for whom it has been prepared."

When the ten disciples heard this, they began to be indignant with James and John. Jesus called them over and said to them, "You know that those who are regarded as rulers of the Gentiles lord it over them, and those in high positions act as tyrants over them. But it is not so among you. On the contrary, whoever wants to become great among you will be your servant, and whoever wants to be first among you will be a slave to all. For even the Son of Man did not come to be served, but to serve, and to give his life as a ransom for many."

As with the account in chapter 9, the story here in Mark 10 is preceded by Jesus repeating His warning to the disciples that

He would be crucified and raised on the third day. Seemingly unconcerned by their Lord's imminent suffering, the disciples were consumed with their own greatness, mustering the audacity to ask Jesus to sit at His right and left in glory.

In response, Jesus suggested that they didn't understand what they were asking for, and in his questions about His "cup" and His "baptism," Jesus predicted their own suffering and death on His behalf. Following Him is not about platforms or prestigious seats. Rather, following Him is about surrender, sacrifice, and servanthood. The "great ones," according to Jesus, are the servants who "will be a slave to all."

Moving Forward

Other passages provide the same kind of instruction (see Matt. 23 and Luke 22). Christ has called us to a life of humility and servanthood. When I read these words from our Lord, I have great concern over my own and my fellow ministers' state. My prayer moving forward is that God will clarify in each of our hearts His calling, giving us the wisdom to see that servanthood delights Him and brings life for us. Everything else will pass away.

Note
1. Saint Augustine, *Confessions* (New York, Penguin: 1961), book 1, chapter 1.

Part 2

What Does Servanthood Look Like?

What does servanthood look like? Chapters 3 through 5 look closely at various biblical examples of servants. We could analyze servanthood in different ways, but as believers, followers, and ministers of the gospel, we should be most concerned with what the Bible has to say. Whereas part 1 set the context for servanthood by looking at the conditions of our world and the ways ministers can become prideful and egocentric, these next three chapters explore what the Bible teaches us about servanthood.

We begin in chapter 3 with biblical examples found in the patriarchs, the prophets, and the apostles, including Abraham, Moses, David, Isaiah, Paul, and Peter. In each of these men's stories, we will notice common themes about their character and lives that allow us to describe them as servants. They all embodied a specific set of virtues: humility, obedience, sacrifice, trust, and devotion.

We turn in chapter 4 to the best example of all, Jesus Christ Himself. Starting with Isaiah's "Servant Songs," which foretell of the Servant Messiah who would come, and then examining these prophecies' fulfillment in the Gospel accounts of Jesus Christ, we find that Christ was a servant for us and for His Father. And in His servanthood, Jesus models for us what we should be. We not only discover the same set of virtues in Jesus—humility, obedience, sacrifice, trust, and devotion—but we find their clearest and best expression of them.

Part 2 concludes in chapter 5 with a closer exploration of the virtues identified in chapters 3 and 4. As we unpack those virtues, we will first examine the concept of a virtue itself to uncover the impact that virtues have on us and the people around us. Servants, I argue, are people who embody all five virtues.

Chapter 3

Servanthood throughout the Bible

In the last two chapters we explored the brokenness of the world and the factors that turn humble servants into people who are egocentric and self-centered. The resolution to these problems is found in cultivating the character of a servant. So we turn our attention next to what the Bible has to say about the call to servanthood. In this chapter we will identify several important biblical themes worthy of our consideration, beginning in the Old Testament with the lives of saints such as Abraham, Moses, David, Isaiah, and several others. In each case, despite their mistakes and failures, these leaders were characterized by humility, obedience, sacrifice, trust, and devotion. As such, God identified them as servants.

We will also consider several New Testament figures, noting how they embraced the characteristics of servanthood as well.

Along the way, I hope you will see that servanthood is a clear theme in the lives of God's people in both the Old and New Testaments. We cannot follow Christ without a posture of servanthood. Servanthood is on display in the lives of those God used in mighty kingdom ways, and it remains essential to our life and calling today. This journey through the lives of biblical figures will demonstrate certain characteristics of a servant, such as humility, obedience, sacrifice, trust, and devotion, that we will discuss in more detail in a future chapter.

Servanthood among the Old Testament Saints

Abraham

We begin with Abraham. He is called a servant by God in Genesis 26:24 when the Lord appears to Isaac, reassuring Isaac that He is with him. The Bible says, "The LORD appeared to him that night and said, 'I am the God of your father Abraham. Do not be afraid, for I am with you. I will bless you and multiply your offspring because of my servant Abraham." We start with Abraham, not because he was perfect but because he is a good example of the humility, obedience, sacrifice, trust, and devotion that characterize a servant of God. We also begin with him because in him we have a clear picture of how God uses imperfect servants for major kingdom purposes.

Consider two pivotal moments in Abraham's life. The first came in Genesis 12 when God called Abraham to leave his father's house and go to a foreign land, and the second came when God commanded him to sacrifice Isaac, his promised son. Hebrews 11:8–12, 17–19 (NIV) says:

> By faith Abraham, when called to go to a place he would later receive as his inheritance, obeyed and went, even though he did not know where he was going. By faith he made his home in the promised land like a stranger in a foreign country; he lived in tents, as did Isaac and Jacob, who were heirs with him of the same promise. For he was looking forward to the city with foundations, whose architect and builder is God. And by faith even Sarah, who was past childbearing age, was enabled to bear children because she considered him faithful who had made the promise. And so from this one man, and he as good as dead, came descendants as numerous as the stars in the sky and as countless as the sand on the seashore. . . .

By faith Abraham, when God tested him, offered Isaac as a sacrifice. He who had embraced the promises was about to sacrifice his one and only son, even though God had said to him, "It is through Isaac that your offspring will be reckoned." Abraham reasoned that God could even raise the dead, and so in a manner of speaking he did receive Isaac back from death.

Abraham made his share of mistakes and struggled at times to trust God. Nevertheless, God used him to establish the Jewish people and to inaugurate His plan of salvation that culminated in Jesus Christ. Why did God use him? Because Abraham was a faithful servant, exemplifying humility, obedience, sacrifice, trust, and devotion in the way he followed God. He trusted God when called upon to do unthinkable things. He willingly offered God the sacrifice of obedience by leaving his father and family and by his willingness to sacrifice Isaac. Rightly so, Abraham became an example of a servant of God, helping us to see what dispositions God wants in us.

Moses

Moses is another important example of a figure in the Old Testament who embodied servanthood. Moses's life is both fascinating and central to Judaism and Christianity. After hearing the cry of His people and remembering His promise to Abraham in Exodus 2:24, God called Moses to serve Him by confronting Pharaoh and leading Israel out of Egypt. In Exodus 3:9–10, God said to Moses, "Because the Israelites' cry for help has come to me, and I have also seen the way the Egyptians are oppressing them, therefore, go. I am sending you to Pharaoh so that you may lead my people, the Israelites, out of Egypt."

Moses struggled to trust God in the initial moments of this calling, but as the book of Exodus and the entire Pentateuch make clear, Moses was obedient to the Lord and did what he was called to do. As a result, he is called God's servant in Exodus 14:31, after he brought the children of Israel out of Egypt and through the Red Sea. He is called a servant again in Deuteronomy 34:5 near the end of his life. A servant to both God and Israel, Moses is used by God to deliver His people from Pharaoh's bondage, to give the Law to God's people, and also to serve as Israel's most important prophet. In moments where the people rebelled against God and caused His anger to burn against them, Moses stood between God and man, pleading for God's mercy and calling on God to remember His promises to Abraham, Isaac, and Jacob (Exod. 32:11–14).

Moses obeyed instead of making his life about himself. On behalf of God and His people, Moses forsook the luxuries and comforts of Egypt, yielded to God's will, and was used by

God to liberate His people from the most powerful man in the world at that time. Hebrews 11:24–29 (NIV) says:

> By faith Moses, when he had grown up, refused to be known as the son of Pharaoh's daughter. He chose to be mistreated along with the people of God rather than to enjoy the fleeting pleasures of sin. He regarded disgrace for the sake of Christ as of greater value than the treasures of Egypt, because he was looking ahead to his reward. By faith he left Egypt, not fearing the king's anger; he persevered because he saw him who is invisible. By faith he kept the Passover and the application of blood, so that the destroyer of the firstborn would not touch the firstborn of Israel.
>
> By faith the people passed through the Red Sea as on dry land; but when the Egyptians tried to do so, they were drowned.

The author of Hebrews specifically notes the cost of Moses's obedience to God. Instead of living a life filled with pleasure and ease, Moses set it all aside as an act of worship, choosing to give himself in service to the one true God.

Like Abraham, Moses wasn't perfect. There were times when his anger got the best of him, and he resisted doing what

God called him to do. Also, like Abraham, Moses embodied the characteristics of a servant. Specifically, in the moments described above, and in many more, Moses exhibited humility, obedience, sacrifice, trust, and devotion. When all was said and done, he was faithful to do what God called him to do. He forsook comfort and luxury, and he trusted God to do what only God can do.

David

King David is described as a servant in numerous places. In 2 Samuel 7:5, for example, God said to Nathan, "Go to my servant David and say, 'This is what the LORD says: Are you to build me a house to dwell in?'" In addition to asking David about building a temple, God also promised in 2 Samuel to establish David's throne forever. Reflecting on God's promise in this passage, Psalm 89:19–29 recounts what God had to say to David.

> I have granted help to a warrior;
> I have exalted one chosen from the people.
> I have found David my servant;
> I have anointed him with my sacred oil.
> My hand will always be with him,
> and my arm will strengthen him.
> The enemy will not oppress him;
> the wicked will not afflict him.

I will crush his foes before him
and strike those who hate him.
My faithfulness and love will be with him,
and through my name
his horn will be exalted.
I will extend his power to the sea
and his right hand to the rivers.
He will call to me, "You are my Father,
my God, the rock of my salvation."
I will also make him my firstborn,
greatest of the kings of the earth.
I will always preserve my faithful love for
him,
and my covenant with him will endure.
I will establish his line forever,
his throne as long as heaven lasts.

David is described as a warrior because he defeated Goliath, the Philistines, and many more. Yet it wasn't David's willingness to fight for God that we should notice. The Bible is clear that God saw in David a man after His own heart. After King Saul's rebellion, God set circumstances in motion to remove Saul and replace him with someone who would have a heart for God and His kingdom. Through Samuel, God said to Saul, "The LORD has found a man after his own heart, and the

LORD has appointed him as ruler over his people, because you have not done what the LORD commanded" (1 Sam. 13:14). Then, in 1 Samuel 16:10–13, God revealed that David was the servant He sought.

> After Jesse presented seven of his sons to him, Samuel told Jesse, "The LORD hasn't chosen any of these." Samuel asked him, "Are these all the sons you have?"
>
> "There is still the youngest," he answered, "but right now he's tending the sheep." Samuel told Jesse, "Send for him. We won't sit down to eat until he gets here." So Jesse sent for him. He had beautiful eyes and healthy, handsome appearance.
>
> Then the LORD said, "Anoint him, for he is the one." So Samuel took the horn of oil and anointed him in the presence of his brothers, and the Spirit of the LORD came powerfully on David from that day forward.

Several of the most important qualities of a servant are found in King David. In particular, he was humble, obedient, and full of devotion to God. While this description may not fit what we would expect in a king, it was exactly what God wanted. Even David's father, Jesse, failed to understand the kind of person God sought as king. God's ideal person was not the largest, strongest, oldest, or even the most established. Rather, God sought someone simple, unassuming, and focused on doing His work. David's devotion to God shaped everything in his life, causing him to be humble and leading him to obedience.

The Prophets

Before turning to the New Testament, let's look quickly at the prophets as well. In Isaiah 20:3; 2 Kings 17:13; and Jeremiah 26:5, the prophets are referred to collectively as God's servants. Considering many of their lives and service to God, it is easy to see why God thinks of them this way. Like Abraham, Moses, and David, they were characterized by humility, obedience, sacrifice, trust, and devotion. The prophet Micah, for example, reminded us of the need for humility by saying that God has shown us "what is good and what it is the LORD requires of you: to act justly, to love faithfulness, and to walk humbly with your God" (Mic. 6:8).

Daniel also exemplified the qualities of a servant we have observed—humility, obedience, sacrifice, trust, and devotion. In Daniel 2, Daniel and his friends Shadrach, Meshach, and Abed-Nego were promoted to seats of honor and power. In the next chapter, they would face an immediate test of their faith. In chapter 3, Nebuchadnezzar made an image of gold that was ninety feet high, commanding all citizens to bow down before it in worship. As devoted servants of God, this was not something Daniel and his friends were willing to do. Because of their refusal, Nebuchadnezzar would attempt to have them killed by throwing them into the fiery furnace. Daniel 3:15–18 records his threat and the response of Daniel's friends.

> "Now if you're ready, when you hear the sound of the horn, flute, zither, lyre, harp, drum, and every kind of music, fall down and worship the statue I made. But if you don't worship it, you will immediately be thrown into a furnace of blazing fire—and who is the god who can rescue you from my power?"
>
> Shadrach, Meshach, and Abednego replied to the king, "Nebuchadnezzar, we don't need to give you an answer to this question. If the God we serve exists, then he can rescue us from the furnace of blazing fire, and he can rescue us from the power of you, the king. But even if he does not rescue us, we want you as king to know that we will not serve your gods or worship the gold statue you set up."

Notice the character of Daniel's friends. These men are not only humble; they are also obedient to God above all others, willing to sacrifice their lives for that obedience, full of devotion and trust in God.

We see these same characteristics in Daniel in chapter 6. While Daniel held a prominent place in Darius's kingdom, his enemies devised a trap for him. They convinced the king to sign a law that forbade citizens and inhabitants of the land from praying to anyone other than the king. After it was signed by the king, the Bible records Daniel's response. "When Daniel learned that the document had been signed, he went into his house. The windows in its upstairs room opened toward Jerusalem, and three times a day he got down on his knees, prayed, and gave thanks to his God, just as he had done before" (6:10). Trapped between obedience to God and disobedience to the king, Daniel was thrown into the lion's den, only to find God once again faithful to His servant by sparing his life.

We can learn much from these Old Testament figures. In particular, each of them is an important example of servanthood because of the character they possess. Each of them was marked by humility, obedience, sacrifice, trust, and devotion.

Servanthood among the New Testament Saints

The New Testament develops the theme of servanthood in much more detail and with greater clarity. While Jesus's apostles described themselves in various ways, they most regularly identified themselves as servants of Jesus Christ. This language is typically seen in their opening greetings at the beginning of their letters. Paul called himself a servant in Romans (1:1), Philippians (1:1), and Titus (1:1), as did James (1:1), Peter (2 Pet. 1:1), and Jude (v. 1). Peter wrote, "Simeon Peter, a servant and an apostle of Jesus Christ: To those who have received a faith equal to ours through the righteousness of our God and Savior Jesus Christ" (2 Pet. 1:1).

The apostles did more than just identify themselves in this way; they also elaborated on what being a servant means. As they described servanthood, we encounter the same characteristics—humility, obedience, sacrifice, trust, and devotion—that we saw in the Old Testament saints. Paul, for example, wrote in 1 Corinthians 4:1–2, "A person should think of us in this way: as servants of Christ and managers of the mysteries of God. In this regard, it is required that managers be found faithful." Paul was clear that people should think of him, and us, as servants. It is the servant's primary responsibility to be found faithful to the work God has called him to do. Five chapters later in 1 Corinthians 9:19–23, Paul wrote:

> Although I am free from all and not anyone's slave, I have made myself a slave to everyone, in order to win more people. To the Jews I became like a Jew, to win Jews; to those under

the law, like one under the law—though I myself am not under the law—to win those under the law. To those who are without the law, like one without the law—though I am not without God's law but under the law of Christ—to win those without the law. To the weak I became weak, in order to win the weak. I have become all things to all people, so that I may by every possible means save some. Now I do all this because of the gospel, so that I may share in the blessings.

As one who had been made free by Jesus Christ, Paul surrendered himself like a servant to all people for the purpose of seeing many come to faith in Jesus. His obedience is given greater clarity in Romans 12:1–2, when Paul appealed to us to give our lives as living sacrifices. He wrote, "Therefore, brothers and sisters, in view of the mercies of God, I urge you to present your bodies as a living sacrifice, holy and pleasing to God; this is your true worship. Do not be conformed to this age, but be transformed by the renewing of your mind, so that you may discern what is the good, pleasing, and perfect will of God."

Throughout the New Testament we find the same characteristics of servanthood in the apostles that we did in the Old Testament saints. Paul and the apostles, as ministers of the gospel, were marked by humility, obedience, sacrifice, trust, and devotion. Though they were apostles, they humbled themselves as servants, obeyed the Lord's calling on their lives, gave their lives as a sacrifice, trusted God in the face of persecution, and modeled devotion to Jesus.

Moving Forward

In this chapter we've traced the theme of servanthood in the Old Testament and New Testament. The patriarchs and the prophets were described as servants, and so were the New Testament apostles. In the next chapter, we take a more focused look at the most important biblical figure of all, Jesus Christ. As we shall see, Jesus, the Suffering Servant, came to serve and give His life as a ransom for many.

Chapter 4

Jesus Christ, the Suffering Servant

Examples of servanthood in the Old Testament and New Testament provide a strong contrast to the greed, pride, and self-centeredness we saw in chapter 1. They counter the applause and platform-seeking ministers we can become if we aren't vigilant.

This chapter explores a far more important example of servanthood, the servant motif that is central to the Messiah Himself. It considers the life and ministry of Jesus Christ, whom the Old Testament sets forth as the Suffering Servant. We look at prophecies of the Suffering Servant found in Isaiah and how they are fulfilled in Jesus Christ in the New Testament. In this exploration, we cannot escape that servanthood is central to who Jesus Christ is, His life and ministry.

We must therefore aspire to it ourselves as we seek to follow Him.

The Suffering Servant

The Bible applies the term *servant* to a variety of people in a variety of roles. For example, the term may refer to slaves from defeated enemies, hired servants, devoted followers of Jesus, soldiers in the military, or anyone who serves in a given capacity. As we saw in the last chapter, some of the most important biblical figures are described as servants. In Isaiah, we are introduced to the most important servant of all, the one who would ultimately suffer for our sins, bringing redemption to God's people and ushering in the kingdom of God.

Early prophecies about Jesus are examples of the servant motif that began in the Old Testament but find fulfillment in Him. The prophets described a servant who would bring redemption and grace to God's people, and the apostles pointed to Jesus as the one who fulfilled this role. Since both Testaments point us to Jesus Christ, they also show us that servanthood was central to who He is and to what His life and ministry are about.

In the book of Isaiah, scholars note four key passages about the "servant of the Lord": 42:1–9; 49:1–13; 50:4–11; and 52:13–53:12. Taken as messianic descriptions of Jesus Christ, these passages show us various ways Christ fulfills the Father's purposes and serves God's people by offering redemption. In the first Servant Song, Isaiah 42, God identifies His servant whom He has chosen. Here God notes that His servant will bring justice to the earth and provide strength for the weak. He says, "I have put my Spirit on him; he will bring justice to the nations. He will not cry out or shout or make his voice heard in the streets. He will not break a bruised reed, and he will not put out a smoldering wick; he will faithfully bring justice" (42:1–3). Where injustice reigns, God's servant will bring justice. References to bruised reeds and smoldering wicks refer to the weak, the poor, and the marginalized, or those many people would treat as throwaways, insignificant and unworthy of our attention. Yet the Messiah will not treat them this way. He will give them hope and strength. He will treat them with love and grace.

The Lord assures us of His commitment to help His chosen Servant accomplish these things by saying, "I am the Lord. I have called you for a righteous purpose, and I will hold you by your hand. I will watch over you, and I will appoint you to be a covenant for the people and a light to the nations, in order to open blind eyes, to bring out prisoners from the dungeon, and those sitting in darkness from the prison house" (42:6–7). In this Servant Song, we are assured that God's Messiah will serve the poor, the marginalized, and the downtrodden by giving them strength and hope and by bringing justice where injustice dominates our lives.

In Isaiah 49:1–13, the second Servant Song, God speaks again of His steadfast commitment to help the servant accomplish His work of redemption and bring hope to those who are afflicted. As the Israelites expected, the Servant would offer redemption to Israel and the tribes of Jacob. But He will also do much more. He will bring hope and salvation "for the nations." In verse 6, for example, the Lord says to the servant, "It is not enough for you to be my servant raising up the tribes of Jacob and restoring the protected ones of Israel. I will also make you a light for the nations, to be my salvation to the ends of the earth."

Incredibly important to our theology and understanding of the Messiah, Christ, the Servant of the Lord, is that He brings salvation and hope not just to the Hebrew people but to all the peoples of the earth. In this respect, Isaiah prophesies the fulfillment of Genesis 12:1–3 where God called Abraham and gave him a promise for all the nations. The Lord said to Abraham, "Go from your land, your relatives, and your father's house to the land that I will show you. I will make you into a great nation, I will bless you, I will make your name great, and you will be a blessing. I will bless those who bless you, I will curse anyone who treats you with contempt, and all the peoples on earth will be blessed through you."

We see that God's promises of hope and salvation were not just for the Jewish people but also for the Gentiles and the nations. Isaiah indicates to us that God had not forgotten His promise to the nations and that His Servant, the Messiah, would bring it to fulfillment.

In Isaiah 50:1–11, we find the third song about God's Servant. The servant motif takes on an additional feature in this passage. We learn how He will bring salvation to the weary and broken, both in Israel and among the nations. He will do it through His own suffering. In Isaiah 50:4–6, the Servant speaks of the Lord's instruction to Him and His commitment to die for our salvation.

> The Lord God has given me
> the tongue of those who are instructed
> to know how to sustain the weary with a
>   word.
> He awakens me each morning;
> he awakens my ear to listen like those being
>   instructed.
> The Lord God has opened my ear,
> and I was not rebellious;
> I did not turn back.
> I gave my back to those who beat me,

and my cheeks to those who tore out my
    beard.
I did not hide my face from scorn and
    spitting.

The Servant gives Himself to "sustain the weary with a word" and accomplishes salvation for them through His suffering. He does not turn back from the beatings, the strikes against Him, or from those who mock Him and spit on Him. In Isaiah's third song about the Servant, we see that He is not just a servant, but He is a *suffering* servant who gives His life for broken people like you and me.

The fourth Servant Song is found in Isaiah 52:13–53:12. In this song, humility and suffering become more prominent in the servant motif. Isaiah 53:2–3 describes the humble nature of the servant, saying,

> "He grew up before him like a young plant and like a root out of dry ground. He didn't have an impressive form or majesty that we should look at him, no appearance that we should desire him. He was despised and rejected by men, a man of suffering who knew what sickness was. He was like someone people turned away from; he was despised, and we didn't value him."

How ironic and stunning. The one who created and made the world (John 1:1–5) is now met with such little esteem and respect. He created the people who looked away from Him and had no desire for Him.

Yet Isaiah shows us that the irony is far more drastic than that. The one who made the universe would not just be rejected; He would suffer and be destroyed for our transgressions. Isaiah 52:14, for example, predicts that the suffering of the Servant will be so great that He will be unrecognizable. He says, "Just as many were appalled at you—his appearance was so disfigured that he did not look like a man, and his form did not resemble a human being." As he goes on to explain in Isaiah 53:4–10, the Servant will bear our sins and pay our debt.

> Yet he himself bore our sicknesses,
> and he carried our pains;
> but we in turn regarded him stricken,
> struck down by God, and afflicted.
> But he was pierced because of our rebellion,
> crushed because of our iniquities;
> punishment for our peace was on him,
> and we are healed by his wounds.
> We all went astray like sheep;
> we all have turned to our own way;
> and the LORD has punished him
> for the iniquity of us all.

He was oppressed and afflicted,
yet he did not open his mouth.
Like a lamb led to the slaughter
and like a sheep silent before her shearers,
he did not open his mouth.
He was taken away because of oppression
    and judgment,
and who considered his fate?
For he was cut off from the land of the
    living;
he was struck because of my people's
    rebellion.
He was assigned a grave with the wicked,
but he was with a rich man at his death,
because he had done no violence
and had not spoken deceitfully.

Yet the LORD was pleased to crush him
    severely.
When you make him a guilt offering,
he will see his seed, he will prolong his days,
and by his hand, the LORD's pleasure will be
    accomplished.

This prophecy is stunning in every possible way. It is stunning because Isaiah predicts Christ's suffering in such detail some seven hundred years before His birth. But it is even more stunning to see what Christ, the Suffering Servant, would do for us. As a reward for His sacrifice, the Lord will grant the nations to Him. The Lord promises that "after his anguish, he will see light and be satisfied. By his knowledge, my righteous servant will justify many, and he will carry their iniquities. Therefore I will give him the many as a portion, and he will receive the mighty as spoil" (53:11–12). Furthermore, the Lord promises that "my servant will be successful; he will be raised and lifted up and greatly exalted" (52:13).

Isaiah's Servant Songs are bedrock to our understanding of the Messiah. Here we find that the Messiah will be, in a more sure and full sense than any other biblical figure, marked by humility, obedience, sacrifice, trust, and devotion. This is how Isaiah describes Him. As we will see, this is also how the New Testament portrays Him in the fulfillment of Isaiah's prophesies.

New Testament Fulfillment

Jesus Christ is presented as the fulfillment of Isaiah's Servant Songs in what Jesus says about His own ministry and in what the apostles say about Him. Matthew 12, for example, records a story of Jesus healing a man's hand on the Sabbath and of the Pharisees' outrage at this act of grace. Yet Matthew notes that this is exactly what Isaiah foretold, saying that this was done "so that what was spoken through the prophet Isaiah might be fulfilled" (12:17). In Matthew's mind, the mercy Jesus displays to the sick is exactly the kind of care Isaiah envisions with his reference to smoldering wicks and bruised reeds. Instead of treating such people as unworthy of care and attention, such that they should just be left to die, God's Servant cares for them and extends grace to them. Understandably, Matthew presents Jesus as the long-awaited Servant Messiah.

In Acts 3, Peter and John come to the temple for prayer and encounter a lame man, unable to walk from birth. After the man begs for money from Peter and John, Peter responds with the grace and power of Jesus. "'I don't have silver or gold, but what I do have, I give you: In the name of Jesus Christ of Nazareth, get up and walk!' Then, taking him by the right hand he raised him up, and at once his feet and ankles became strong. So he jumped up and started to walk, and he entered the temple with them—walking, leaping, and praising God" (Acts 3:6–8).

Needless to say, the people who witnessed this miracle were astonished and amazed at what Peter was able to do for the man. In response, Peter seized the moment to preach Christ as the fulfillment of all that was prophesied by Isaiah and the other prophets.

"Fellow Israelites, why are you amazed at this? Why do you stare at us, as though we had made him walk by our own power or godliness? The God of Abraham, Isaac, and Jacob, the God of our ancestors, has glorified his servant Jesus, whom you handed over and denied before Pilate, though he had decided to release him. You denied the Holy and Righteous One and asked to have a murderer released to you. You killed the source of life, whom God raised from the dead; we are witnesses of this. By faith in his name, his name has made this man strong, whom you see and know. So the faith that comes through Jesus has given him this perfect health in front of all of you." (Acts 3:12–16)

He then added, "In this way God fulfilled what he had predicted through all the prophets—that his Messiah would suffer" (Acts 3:18). Once again, it is clear that the apostles understood Jesus to be the fulfillment of all that was predicted of the servant Messiah in Isaiah's Servant Songs.

The apostles were not alone in connecting Jesus to the Servant in Isaiah. Jesus made the connection Himself. In Luke 4, for example, Jesus entered the synagogue and read from the Isaiah scroll. Luke says, "He found the place where it was written: The Spirit of the Lord is on me, because he has anointed me to preach good news to the poor. He has sent me to proclaim release to the captives and recovery of sight to the blind, to set free the oppressed, to proclaim the year of the Lord's favor" (Luke 4:17–19). As Jesus finished reading, everyone in the synagogue had their eyes fixed on Him, and He said, "Today as you listen, this Scripture has been fulfilled" (Luke 4:21). The passage Jesus read is from Isaiah 61, but it included an allusion to Isaiah 49:8 in its reference to the "acceptable year of the LORD" (Isa. 61:2 NKJV). Jesus wanted His listeners to understand that He was the long-awaited Messiah whom Isaiah and the other prophets had predicted.

The Gospel writers provide further examples in Jesus's life where He embodied servanthood, such as John's record of Jesus washing the disciples' feet. Whereas this duty was typically reserved for the lowest servant in the house, Jesus took the towel and basin and washed their feet himself (John 13:1–11). What we should notice in this story is not just that it displays the kind of servanthood envisioned by Isaiah but also that it has implications for us as Jesus's followers. As He sat with His disciples after washing their feet, Jesus said, "Do you know what I have done for you? You call me Teacher and Lord—and you are speaking rightly, since that is what I am. So if I, your Lord and Teacher, have washed your feet, you also ought to wash one another's feet. For I have given you an

example, that you also should do just as I have done for you"
(John 13:12–15).

In this moment and many others, Jesus made clear to His
disciples that He was a servant and that He intended those
who follow Him to be servants as well. As a servant, He exemplified humility, obedience, sacrifice, trust, and devotion. He
embodied these virtues so perfectly that He endured the cross,
fulfilling the Father's will and bringing salvation to us. Christ
is thus the model of servanthood whom we should fix our eyes
upon more than any other.

Moving Forward

The Servant Songs, and the New Testament's fulfillment
of them, are central to understanding who Jesus Christ is. But
they are also central to understanding our calling and who
we are supposed to be as His followers. In the Songs, Isaiah
speaks of our Messiah and Savior as a servant. He came not
just for Israel but also for the Gentiles. He came for the broken, the weary, the downtrodden, and sinners like you and
me. He serves us by proclaiming the Lord's mercy and grace
to us. He serves us by sacrificing Himself for us. He serves us
in the humility required of Him by stooping from the throne
of glory to take a lowly form that no one esteemed or desired.
He serves us in His obedience to the Father who sent Him

to bring justice and redemption to the nations. If we cannot see this servanthood in Him, then we do not understand who He is. And if we cannot see that He calls us to follow Him in this posture of servanthood, then we do not understand what being His disciple means. If we cannot bring ourselves to humbly obey Him, then perhaps our lives are mere shadows of something like Christianity rather than the real thing.

I must confess that as I follow Christ through the pages of Scripture, both Old and New Testaments, I am brokenhearted by how dissimilar I am to Him. Yet I must also confess that I find a joyous hope in finding Him in these prophesies and fulfillments. The Servant Isaiah described as the one who brought grace and redemption brought it for me as well. His grace is enough not only to forgive my sins but also to change my sinful heart and reshape me into His beautiful image. This is the hope of our merciful Lord. The one who exposes the ugliness of our soul is the same one who heals us and makes us new again. I may not yet be the servant He calls me to be, but He is able to conform me to Himself.

A Servant. That is who He is. And that, my brothers and sisters, is what we are called to be.

Chapter 5

What Does It Mean to Be a Servant?

In the last two chapters, we looked at servanthood through-out the Bible. We began with the patriarchs and prophets in the Old Testament, then considered the apostles in the New Testament. We saw that they were people of a particular kind of character. They were marked by humility, obedience, sacrifice, trust, and devotion. In chapter 4, we focused our attention on Jesus Christ as He was foretold by the prophets in the servant motif and in how the New Testament presents Christ as the fulfillment of that vision. In Him we found not just the same characteristics—humility, obedience, sacrifice, trust, and devotion—but the perfect embodiment of them.

We now look at those characteristics in greater detail. As you recall, in the introduction of this book I defined servanthood as follows:

> *Servanthood*—the character that causes us to place others before ourselves, helping where people have need, and finding joy in a life focused on others.

What is most important about this view of servanthood is that it is rooted in a particular kind of character. Discussions about character focus on the qualities a person possesses. Put another way, discussions about character are really what we tend to think of as virtues. Servanthood is marked by the virtues of humility, obedience, sacrifice, trust, and devotion. A servant has these virtues and is willing to place others before self, help where people have need, and find joy in a life that is focused on others. In what follows below, we will take a closer look at what virtue is. We will then explore the virtues of humility, obedience, sacrifice, trust, and devotion in detail.

What Is Virtue?

When we hear the word *virtue*, we most likely think of the field of ethics or what it means to be a good person. Because of the way we typically conceive of ethics and morality, we might be inclined to think virtues are about keeping rules. Indeed, certain approaches to ethics and morality view virtue in this way. But this is not what virtue actually is. Rather, discussions about virtues are about the kinds of characteristics a person possesses. Virtues, then, are good characteristics of a person.

Virtues are typically considered in contrast to their negative counterpart—vices. Vices and virtues are both characteristics, but a vice is a negative characteristic that creates destruction in a person's life. If a person has a vice, he will face trouble and difficulty because of that vice, and so will everyone around him.

For example, consider how things tend to go for someone with the vice of alcoholism. An alcoholic may struggle to hold a job, keep healthy relationships, and stay out of trouble. The vice produces difficulty for the person and for those who depend on him. When a dad loses his job because of alcohol, it is bad not just for the father; it is also debilitating for his wife and children. Or consider the vice of pride. The person with this characteristic may find himself looked over for jobs, may have difficulty in his relationships, and may not be thought well of by those around him. In short, vices are negative characteristics that create problems for those who have them and for those under their influence.

Just as a vice is a characteristic or quality, so is a virtue. But a virtue is a positive characteristic. It creates well-being, health, and favor for the one who possesses it and for those influenced by the one who possesses it. Take, for example, the characteristic of courage. The courageous person will face difficulty instead of avoiding it, choosing to deal with problems rather than ignore them and let them fester. As a result of this willingness to be courageous and do hard things, the person with courage creates a better situation for himself and those around him.

Or consider the virtue of honesty. The honest person is willing to tell the truth as opposed to lie, even if the truth is less convenient or stressful. Because he tells the truth, he earns a reputation of being honest, winning the trust and confidence of those around him. As a result of this trust, he is given favor, creating a better situation for himself and those who depend on him. Virtues, then, are positive characteristics that produce well-being, health, or favor in some way.

The Virtues of a Christian Servant

In earlier chapters we discovered that the patriarchs, prophets, apostles, and Jesus Himself were marked by a particular set of characteristics: humility, obedience, sacrifice, trust, and devotion. These characteristics are the virtues of a Christian servant. There may be other virtues worthy of our consideration as well, but these five are foundational and easy to identify in the lives of God's servants. We will consider each one in turn in the rest of this chapter.

Humility

There is no servanthood without humility. Unless we are willing to lower ourselves and surrender our will, we will never take the posture of a servant. Humility is central to the concept of servanthood because a servant is someone who yields his desires and position for the sake of others. When a person is humble, he doesn't seek the attention of others, insist on things being done his way, pretend to be more than he really is, or brag about his accomplishments. Such things are evidence of the vice of pride, and this vice only brings destruction into our lives. By contrast, the person who takes a lower view of his importance reaps the benefit of humility that is life-giving.

We saw this virtue clearly in the lives of the saints considered in chapter 2 and even more clearly in Jesus Himself. David, for example, was a simple shepherd boy whom no one esteemed, including his own father. David wasn't the oldest or strongest of his brothers, and he certainly wasn't the most experienced. Instead, he was a humble shepherd who was faithful in his work. While men looked for something more prestigious, God saw David's heart and elevated him to the throne of Israel.

Paul is also an example of humility. Unlike David, Paul was a highly esteemed Pharisee who held a level of prominence. Nevertheless, Paul exemplified humility. Though he once held a position of great importance, he stepped away from it and yielded his life as a servant to Jesus Christ.

Most clearly, we see humility in the life of Jesus. Paul reflects on Jesus's humility in Philippians 2:6–8, noting that Jesus "who, existing in the form of God, did not consider equality with God as something to be exploited. Instead he emptied himself by assuming the form of a servant, taking on the likeness of humanity. And when he had come as a man, he humbled himself by becoming obedient to the point of death—even to death on a cross."

Humility is not just life-giving; it is also sought in us by the Lord. God's focus on humility is found throughout the Bible but is especially clear in Isaiah 66:2: "I will look favorably on this kind of person: one who is humble, submissive in spirit, and trembles at my word." According to Proverbs 3:34, "He mocks those who mock but gives grace to the humble," and in James 4:10 we are told to "humble [ourselves] before the Lord, and he will exalt [us]."

The Lord loves humility in His people. As we consider what it means to be a servant, we should start with this virtue.

Obedience

There can be no servanthood without obedience to God's will. A servant exists to do the will of another. In the case of Christian servants, it is God's will that we seek to do. Obedience is a virtue that submits our will to God's, allowing His wisdom to work itself out in our lives. In believing that he knows better than God, the disobedient person is cut off from the blessings that can only come from the provision and kindness of God. But an obedient person will heed the instructions and desires of the Lord and bring his life into submission to Him, allowing God's favor to flow into his life.

Many examples of obedience can be found throughout the Bible, including in the lives of those figures covered in previous chapters. Abraham displayed obedience when he answered God's call to him to "go from your land, your relatives, and your father's house to the land that I will show you" (Gen. 12:1). This act of obedience required him to leave everything he knew, everything that gave him confidence, and to leave his family behind. As he responded to God, he brought his life into full submission to the will of God.

In Jesus we again find the clearest and best expression of obedience. A beautiful depiction of his obedience is recorded in Matthew 26:36–46 as Jesus prayed in the garden of Gethsemane. Anticipating His eventual betrayal, trial, beatings, and crucifixion, Jesus prayed, "My Father, if it is possible, let this cup pass from me. Yet not as I will, but as you will" (v. 39). Reflecting on this moment, the author of Hebrews says: "During his earthly life, he offered prayers and appeals with loud cries and tears to the one who was able to save him from death, and he was heard because of his reverence. Although he was the Son, he learned obedience from what he suffered. After he was perfected, he became the source of eternal salvation for all who obey him, and he was declared by God a high priest according to the order of Melchizedek" (Heb. 5:7–11).

In Romans 5:18–19, Paul reminds us that Jesus's obedience brings salvation and redemption. He writes,

> "So then, as through one trespass there is condemnation for everyone, so also through one righteous act there is justification leading to life for everyone. For just as through one man's disobedience the many were made sinners, so also through the one man's obedience the many will be made righteous."

The virtue of obedience is pleasing to the Father. Just as He was pleased by Christ's obedience, He is pleased by ours as well. In 1 Samuel 15, Saul disobeyed the Lord's direct instructions by not destroying all the Amalekites. Saul's reasons for disobedience sound reasonable enough, but in response to

Saul, God says, "Does the LORD take pleasure in burnt offerings and sacrifices as much as in obeying the LORD? Look: to obey is better than sacrifice, to pay attention is better than the fat of rams" (1 Sam. 15:22). Above everything else Saul could have given God, God desired obedience.

In 1 John 5:2–3, John tells us our obedience is proof of our love for God. He says, "This is how we know that we love God's children: when we love God and obey his commands. For this is what love for God is: to keep his commands. And his commands are not a burden." Jesus says the same in John 14:15: "If you love me, you will keep my commands."

Sacrifice

Servanthood also requires sacrifice. The servant is one who gives up something, sometimes even things that are important to him, for the sake of serving God and helping others. It is a virtue because it represents a state of being, or characteristic, that as painful as it may be will always yield gracious fruit from the Lord. When we yield to the Lord's will in faithful obedience, typically there are associated costs. It may cost us time, money, a career path, certain relationships, or, in some cases, our lives. Yet in the offering we find a greater joy than what the things we sacrificed could have given us. We find a satisfaction the world could never produce in our lives.

Moses is a good example of one whose obedience came with great sacrifice. In Hebrews 11:24–29, the author reminds us of what he gave up to obey the Lord. He says, "By faith Moses, when he had grown up, refused to be known as the son of Pharaoh's daughter. He chose to be mistreated along with the people of God rather than to enjoy the fleeting pleasures of sin" (11:24–25 NIV). Yet Moses's sacrifice reminds us of what was just noted in the previous paragraph. In sacrificing such luxuries, Moses found greater pleasures in Christ Himself.

The author of Hebrews writes, "He regarded disgrace for the sake of Christ as of greater value than the treasures of Egypt, because he was looking ahead to his reward. By faith he left Egypt, not fearing the king's anger; he persevered because he saw him who is invisible" (11:26–27 NIV). Instead of keeping his position of prominence and comfort in Egypt, Moses chose to identify with the people of God and endure the hardships with them.

Jesus, too, sacrificed Himself on the cross. His sacrifice was greater than any others, and thus His sacrifice yielded greater good than any other act in all of history. Paul makes this point clear in Romans 5:6–8, writing,

> "For while we were still helpless, at the right time, Christ died for the ungodly. For rarely will someone die for a just person—though for a good person perhaps someone might

even dare to die. But God proves his own
love for us in that while we were still sinners,
Christ died for us."

Likewise, in Romans 12:1, Paul explains that we are called
to sacrifice our lives as an act of worship to Christ. He writes,
"Therefore, brothers and sisters, in view of the mercies of God,
I urge you to present your bodies as a living sacrifice, holy and
pleasing to God; this is your true worship." This description
of our calling comes after Paul's long exploration of God's
salvation for us in chapters 1–11. In light of what Christ has
sacrificed for us, a sacrificial love for Him is the only logical
thing we could give with our lives. While laying down our
lives comes with a cost, it also comes with indescribable joy.

When Christ called the disciples into His service, he was
clear about the cost that would come with it. But He was also
clear about the reward. In Luke 9:24–25, Jesus said to them,
"For whoever wants to save his life will lose it, but whoever
loses his life because of me will save it. For what does it benefit
someone if he gains the whole world, and yet loses or forfeits
himself?" Jesus teaches explicitly here what Moses found to be
true—the joys of our sacrifices outweigh what we give up. The
virtue of sacrifice, then, pleases the Father, but like the other
virtues, it also produces blessedness and joy that only Christ
can give.

Trust

One interesting aspect of the servant's character is that he or she must trust in God. Trust is a virtue, and when placed in the proper person or object, it yields the joyful fruit of God's favor. A servant of God is often placed in difficult, even excruciating, situations. God's servants will face hardships, slow progress, pressure, and pain. There will be moments in the servant's life when he will not sense God's presence and will not understand how the moment fits into the providential plan of God. In those moments the servant must simply trust the Lord. This is the easiest thing in the world to say, but it is often the hardest thing to do. Yet the one who trusts and waits for the Lord will find God to be faithful again and again. She will find that God never forsakes His people, never forgets His promises, and always provides for those who serve Him.

Abraham is a great example of a servant who had to trust the Lord. In Genesis 22, God called Abraham to sacrifice his promised son, Isaac. Abraham and Sarah had long waited for the Lord to fulfill His promise to them, the promise of a son through whom all the nations of the earth would be blessed (Gen. 12:1–3). Then God told Abraham to take Isaac to Mount Moriah and sacrifice him. There was absolutely nothing about this command that made sense to Abraham or to us. It seemed to betray the promises God made to Abraham, promises that were meant to bless Abraham and to bring about the chosen Messiah. In addition, the command was excruciating, to say nothing of the troubling theological questions it brings to mind about God.

Despite all of this, Abraham did what God told him to do. He set forth to the mountain, built an altar, laid Isaac upon that alter, and raised his knife to slay his promised son. What in the world was going through his mind in that moment just before God intervened? The author of Hebrews tells us: "Abraham reasoned that God could even raise the dead, and so in a manner of speaking he did receive Isaac back from death" (11:19 NIV). In other words, Abraham simply trusted God. He trusted Him when nothing made sense, when obedience hurt, and even when God Himself seemed irrational. He trusted. Specifically, the author of Hebrews writes that Abraham trusted Isaac was still God's plan for the bloodline of Jesus and that God would raise Isaac up to accomplish His purposes.

Trust is typified perfectly in Jesus Christ, especially in the moments of His death. As Christ hung on the cross dying, He commended Himself to the Father and put His life in the Father's hands. With a clear reference to Psalm 31:1–5, Luke writes in his Gospel: "It was now about noon, and darkness came over the whole land until three, because the sun's light failed. The curtain of the sanctuary was split down the middle. And Jesus called out with a loud voice, 'Father, into

77

your hands I entrust my spirit.' Saying this, he breathed his last" (Luke 23:44–46).

Just as the psalmist called out in trust to God in moments of grief and agony, Christ likewise put His spirit in the Father's hands, trusting that He would accomplish His will through death. Jesus's trust in the Father was perfect, and it allowed Him to offer Himself as the sacrifice for our sin.

Like Christ, Abraham, and all the servants of old who were marked by the virtue of trust, the Bible makes clear that God calls us to do the same. In Proverbs 3:5–6, for example, God instructs us to "trust in the LORD with all your heart, and do not rely on your own understanding; in all your ways know him, and he will make your paths straight." In Matthew 6:33, after addressing our tendency to worry, Jesus tells us to "seek first the kingdom of God and his righteousness, and all these things will be provided for you." Trust is an essential virtue to the servant of God. Without it we cannot do the hard things we are called to do in service to the King.

Devotion

Finally, devotion is also a defining virtue of God's servants. This characteristic may actually be the one most essential to servanthood, such that it holds all the others together. Moreover, this virtue gives direction to all other virtues in the life of a servant. Humility, obedience, sacrifice, and trust may all be present in a person, but their devotion to God ultimately compels them to take up the towel and basin and give their lives as servants. The devout person is one whose loyalties and commitments are singularly focused on the Lord, seeking Him and His kingdom above all else. The person whose heart is set on the Lord wants Him more than anything and will give everything to bring Him satisfaction. Like the other virtues, devotion brings joy and divine favor into our lives.

Such devotion was found in young David as he was "a man after [God's] own heart" (1 Sam. 13:14). David's love for God was pure, and he desired to please and honor Him in all things. Of course, David made mistakes, some very serious, but he nevertheless showed us what devotion looks like in key moments of life.

Jesus's devotion was clear in His steadfast commitment to do the Father's will. Isaiah 50 reminds us of the Messiah's perspective toward God's will, saying, "I have set my face like flint, and I know I will not be put to shame" (Isa. 50:7). Jesus mentioned in various places His commitment to do the will of His Father. In John 6:38, for instance, He said, "I have come down from heaven, not to do my own will, but the will of him who sent me." This clear sense of devotion directed Christ's actions and continues to model servanthood for us.

Moving Forward

Like the other virtues, devotion is central to servanthood. Commenting on the life we now live as redeemed servants of God, Paul reminds us of the devotion that should be evident in us. He writes, "I have been crucified with Christ, and I no longer live, but Christ lives in me. The life I now live in the body, I live by faith in the Son of God, who loved me and gave himself for me" (Gal. 2:20). Christ redeemed us by His blood, and in response, we are now to live fully devoted to Him and no other. Devotion gives direction and focus to all the other virtues of the servant.

Part 3

What Do Servants Do?

What do servants of Christ do? The next part of this book, chapters 6 through 9, is an attempt to answer this important question. We pulled the cover back on our problems in part 1 and looked at servanthood in the Bible in part 2. Now we must put our feet and hands to action and learn how *to be* servants. If we don't, all our consideration of servanthood is for nothing.

Part 3 begins in chapter 6 with a critically important discussion on the servant's longings and satisfaction. I argue that servanthood is impossible unless our heart's desire is found in God. If the world charms and attracts you, you will always seek it and not the Lord. When we learn to find our true delight in Him, we find freedom from the idols of this world and are able to give everything for Him as servants.

Chapter 7 then considers evangelism and proclamation. While servanthood manifests itself in countless actions and habits, it never neglects clear gospel proclamation. I attack either/or approaches to the unsaved that say we should focus either on "showing" Jesus's love or on "preaching the gospel" to them. A both/and approach is necessary.

In chapter 8 we look at the Great Commission. I contend that followers go where Jesus goes and do what He does. Since Christ came into the world to bring the nations to Himself, we should give ourselves to the same mission.

Part 3, and the book itself, ends with chapter 9, where we explore the Bible passage from which this book gets its name. In Philippians 2, Paul reminds us of the great example of Jesus "who, existing in the form of God, did not consider equality with God as something to be exploited" (Phil. 2:6). With the example of Jesus in mind, Paul's primary instruction for us is to "let this mind be in you which was also in Christ Jesus" (Phil. 2:5 NKJV). Our calling is clear and simple: to follow Jesus's example of humility and servanthood, giving ourselves for the sake of others.

A Servant's Longing and Satisfaction

As we have already seen, servanthood is modeled throughout the Scriptures. We observe it in the most important figures of the Bible, especially Jesus. More importantly, the whole canon of Scripture testifies that we are called by God into a life of servanthood. As Christ said to His disciples, "Whoever wants to become great among you will be your servant, and whoever wants to be first among you will be a slave to all. For even the Son of Man did not come to be served, but to serve, and to give his life as a ransom for many" (Mark 10:43–45).

Admittedly, the call to servanthood is costly. A servant lays down his life, his dreams, his desires, and at times even his needs. Jesus was well aware of the cost when He said, "If anyone wants to follow after me, let him deny himself, take up his cross, and follow me." He even compared servanthood to loss of life, speaking about a follower as someone who "loses his life because of me" (Matt. 16:24–25).

In this chapter we focus on what makes a life of sacrifice possible for the servant of God. To become the servant God calls us to be will cost us everything. On the face of it, obedience to God's call seems like all give and no gain. It looks like we lose everything and abandon our own flourishing. How can one give up so much? Jesus did, indeed, talk about losing our lives to follow Him, but He also made clear that "whoever loses his life because of me will find it" (Matt. 16:25). As such, while it may seem that the servant's life is all give and no gain, this is not the case. The servant gains infinitely more than he ever gives up in his service to Christ.

The argument of this chapter is clear: a servant can lay his life down in sacrifice because he finds Christ to be more satisfying and life-giving than anything this world offers. In the eyes of the watching world, a servant's sacrifices may seem foolish and absurd. When unbelievers look at us, they see forsaken opportunities or a wasted life. Our sacrifices for Christ will never make sense to them, as they are often consumed with power, money, and fame, thinking these things satisfy the soul and are worth pursuing. However, we should ignore their perspective and their opinions of a Christian servant's choices because they don't have eyes to see what is valuable or worthy of our heart's devotion.

A Christian servant lays this world down and instead seeks Christ because Christ is better and more satisfying. Once the servant realizes Christ's infinite value, he sees the wisdom in giving up everything to serve Christ and His people. The value and satisfaction of God is a common theme throughout the Bible, found in a countless number of passages. I will focus on three such passages: Psalm 63; Philippians 3; and Matthew 13.

Psalm 63

We begin with Psalm 63, which beautifully describes the worth of God and the delight we find in Him. This theme is found throughout the book of Psalms, and we could consider a great number of them, including Psalms 16; 23; 42; and 90, to name just a few. Psalm 63, however, is one of the clearest expressions of His worth to us. In 63:1–7, the psalmist writes:

> God, you are my God; I eagerly seek you.
> I thirst for you;
> my body faints for you
> in a land that is dry, desolate, and without
>   water.
> So I gaze on you in the sanctuary
> to see your strength and your glory.

My lips will glorify you
because your faithful love is better than life.
So I will bless you as long as I live;
at your name, I will lift up my hands.
You satisfy me as with rich food;
my mouth will praise you with joyful lips.

When I think of you as I lie on my bed,
I meditate on you during the night watches
because you are my helper;
I will rejoice in the shadow of your wings.

Let me highlight two points the psalmist makes. First, notice that God is the satisfaction of the psalmist's heart. This point is subtle but highly important for us to understand. It's not God's provision that is satisfying; it is God Himself. Likewise, it is not God's plan for the psalmist that fulfills him; rather, it is God Himself. If it is merely God's plan or provision we delight in, then God is a mere instrumental good to us. That is, if it is only in His plan and provision that we seek and find delight, then God is nothing more to us than a resource, existing to give us what we want and need.

The psalmist doesn't see God this way. He views God Himself, not just God's plans or provision, as satisfying. In verse 1 he writes, "God, you are my God; I eagerly seek you," and in verse 5, "You satisfy me as with rich food." We should be grateful that God provides for us and has a plan for us, but we miss out on true delight if we misunderstand that God Himself is what we long for most. Nothing else, including important spiritual benefits like His plan and provision, will actually fulfill us. As such, even if things don't work out for us the way we would think they should, we can be content in our communion with God, the one who satisfies.

Second, notice the psalmist's physical description of his desire for God. In verse 1 he writes, "I thirst for you; my body faints for you in a land that is dry, desolate, and without water." The psalmist likens his desire for God to that of deep thirst or hunger. Most of us have never known what real thirst and hunger are like, as we've never had to go without the provisions of food and drink. For someone who is famished and parched, the longing for food and drink is all-consuming, controlling every thought and action. The parched person is truly desperate and will do anything for a drink. I must confess that I have never craved God so desperately. Yet the psalmist did. His desire for God reached the point of desperation and was all-consuming, controlling his every thought and action. The psalmist knew that in God his satisfaction would be found.

Psalm 63 captures an essential truth about servanthood. Earlier I asked how it could be possible for us to give what we've been called to give and to lay down what we have been called to lay down. The cost is steep. Psalm 63 helps us see that our gain is greater still. We may, indeed, be called to give our all in service to God, but we also find in Him the true and better satisfaction we seek. He, and He alone, can satisfy the soul.

As such, only when we find Him will we be freed from our slavery to worldly cravings. The degree to which we still hang on to the charms of this world is the degree to which we are still unsatisfied in Him. When we hold onto our idols, in bondage to their deceptions, we are incapable of finding the joyful freedom found in surrender. Only when we are no longer under the delusion that power, fame, money, and other worldly offerings can satisfy us will we be willing to lay them down and take up the towel and the basin. A servant can give it all because a servant has found it all. Psalm 63 reminds us where our "all" is to be found.

Philippians 3

The apostle Paul seemed to understand what Psalm 63 teaches. He knew that his own personal accomplishments and earthly acclaim were nothing in comparison to the greatness of Christ. He saw that Christ supplies a greater joy, a better hope, and a fuller satisfaction. In Philippians 3, he describes all of this in pointed terms. The background is his concern over the Jewish leaders trying to convince Philippian Christians that they needed circumcision to fulfill the law and please God, as opposed to the grace of Jesus Christ alone. The Jewish leaders, filled with self-confidence in their own personal religious merit, placed their hope in their ability to keep the law. Their hope was not in God's grace, and their joy wasn't either.

They thought they were righteous by keeping the law, but Paul said they had nothing in terms of self-righteousness compared to him. In Philippians 3:4–6, he wrote, "If anyone else thinks he has grounds for confidence in the flesh, I have more: circumcised the eighth day; of the nation of Israel, of the tribe of Benjamin, a Hebrew born of Hebrews; regarding the law, a Pharisee; regarding zeal, persecuting the church; regarding the righteousness that is in the law, blameless." Paul's point was simple: none of the self-righteous Judaizers had the religious credentials he did. In the eyes of the Jews, Paul had attained as much righteousness as anyone possibly could.

The important part of the text, however, comes in what Paul said next. None of this, absolutely none of it, was actually worth anything. As he would remind the Philippian believers, none of his religious credentials gave him merit or joyful satisfaction. By contrast, Christ gives all of this to us. In Philippians 3:7–11, Paul wrote:

> But everything that was a gain to me, I have considered to be a loss because of Christ. More than that, I also consider everything to be a loss in view of the surpassing value

of knowing Christ Jesus my Lord. Because of him I have suffered the loss of all things and consider them as dung, so that I may gain Christ and be found in him, not having a righteousness of my own from the law, but one that is through faith in Christ—the righteousness from God based on faith. My goal is to know him and the power of his resurrection and the fellowship of his sufferings, being conformed to his death, assuming that I will somehow reach the resurrection from among the dead.

Whereas Paul once placed his hope and confidence in who he was and what he had become ("everything that was a gain to me"), he now "considered[ed] everything to be a loss" because of Christ. Now that he had discovered the surpassing beauty, worth, and life-giving grace of Jesus, Paul understood that his own righteousness was worth nothing. It was now a loss to him, having no real value and giving no real joy. Jesus, on the other hand, was worth everything.

Paul goes so far as to say that all those things he once had confidence in, he now considers rubbish. Most of our modern Bible translations soften Paul's meaning with the word choice of "rubbish." The CSB and the KJV, however, come closest to the actual meaning of the Greek word Paul used by translating it as "dung." The Greek word *skybala* can also be translated as "refuse" or "garbage." With this word, Paul likened all his old, religious, self-righteous merit as nothing more than a pile of waste. It wasn't just worthless; it was actually vile and disgusting.

Righteousness that is true and good, pleasing to the Father and life-giving to the soul, cannot be found in what we bring to God. It can only be found in Jesus Christ. Therefore, Paul laid aside all he ever was or sought to be simply to know Jesus and have Him. Knowing and having Christ gives us life. We find in Him all we ever wanted or sought.

Paul found what Jesus said to be true: "Whoever loses his life because of me will find it" (Matt. 16:25). Once Paul knew Christ, he longed to experience not just the power of His resurrection but also the fellowship of His suffering. Like the psalmist, Paul discovered that the joy of knowing Christ and being found in Him brought genuine satisfaction to the soul. Since Christ is worth more than anything we could ever own or achieve for ourselves, we lose nothing in laying everything else down to be His servants. Because of His surpassing worth to us, we can give it all up.

Matthew 13:44–46

Before we close this chapter, we must look at what Jesus had to say about genuine satisfaction. He regularly taught about the kingdom of God. In these teachings, He tried to help the disciples understand how God works, what God cares about, and what is truly valuable in God's kingdom. Matthew 13 lists several of Jesus's most important teachings on the kingdom. He explained the purposes of parables (vv. 10–17), offered the parable of the sower and the seed (13:1–9, 18–23), told the parable of the wheat and the tares (13:24–30, 36–43), and compared the kingdom to a mustard seed that starts small but grows into something large (13:31–32). But I will focus here on His parables about hidden treasure in a field and the pearl of great price. In Matthew 13:44–46, Jesus said:

> "The kingdom of heaven is like treasure, buried in a field, that a man found and reburied. Then in his joy he goes and sells everything he has and buys that field. Again, the kingdom of heaven is like a merchant in search of fine pearls. When he found one priceless pearl, he went and sold everything he had and bought it."

There are two general interpretations of Jesus's parables in Matthew 13. In one view, Jesus is referencing God's perspective on purchasing us for Himself. If this view is correct, then God who finds us, sells all that He has (a reference to giving up Jesus, His Son, on our behalf), and purchases us for Himself. God is thus the one who has found treasure.

Most interpreters, however, suggest the opposite. In this second view, Jesus is speaking of our discovery of unexpected joy. If this view is correct, then we are the ones who find the treasure, and that treasure is nothing other than Christ and His kingdom. We didn't expect to find such treasure, but once we did, we were willing to do the unthinkable and give up everything we own to have Him.

This response makes no sense to those watching. But for those who know what they have found, it is the smartest, most logical, and joyful decision they could ever make. The believer may have "given up everything," but he has found infinite worth in Christ. Interestingly, while Jesus's other parables in chapter 13 each spotlight different ideas related to the kingdom, Jesus doubles up here with two parables that make the same point. The insight of the parable about the pearl of great price is that Christ is worth more to us than everything else we own. To have Him is better than all the riches in the world, and the wise person willingly gives up everything for Christ.

The meaning of Jesus's parables in Matthew 13 could be two directional. They may refer both to God's delight in finding and purchasing us and to our delight in discovering His kingdom and giving everything to follow Christ. However, I believe the second view is correct. Jesus reminds us in these parables of what we have seen in various other places in Scripture. We are called to give our all, to surrender our lives, and to lay everything down for Him.

If that were all there is to the story, then it would be all give and no gain. But there is more to it. When we give our all for Christ, we discover infinite value in Him, so that our sacrifices pale in comparison to His worth and the delight we find in Him. We may give our all, but we find in Him the true delights of our soul that we were made to possess and enjoy.

Christ is the treasure in the field. He is the pearl of great price. When we find Him, we find all we've ever needed and all we've ever wanted. He is the true satisfaction of our souls, and having Him means we have everything. How then can we give our all? We give it because He is better than the rest. Once we taste and see that this is true, no possession we own or aspiration we have in life compares to Him. We experience His worth and are now able to give what we've been called to give.

Until we see this truth and it settles into our hearts, we will never find the freedom to serve Him the way He calls us to serve. All our service will be with half loyalty and partial sacrifice. We will offer parts of ourselves but never the whole. We will always hold out for some benefit, attention, or spotlight that we foolishly think will charm us. Yet once we know, not simply in a cognitive sense but in the depths of our souls, that Christ alone satisfies us, then we will be free to give everything for Him. Like the man who found the treasure in the field or the pearl of great price, we will give everything up to have Him and be found in Him.

Servants and the
Message of the Cross

Servanthood shapes our lives in a vast number of ways. We serve others when we help meet their physical needs. We serve others when we teach them or offer guidance. We serve others when we feed them, care for them medically, or provide them with comfort. Servanthood shows up in big acts of kindness such as these, but it also shows up in small ways with the people who are the closest to us.

I serve my children, for example, when I take extra time to help them with a homework problem. I serve my wife when I offer to cook dinner, do the dishes, fix the car, build a set of bookshelves, or simply lay down my desires for what is in her best interests. Servanthood manifests itself in an almost endless number of ways. Therefore, a chapter that focuses on what a servant does could be longer than anyone would care to read. Suffice it to say that servanthood shows up in virtually every action of our lives.

Because servanthood manifests itself so broadly, the last thing I want to suggest is that there are just one or two ways we primarily serve Jesus. Being a servant applies to everything we do. Yet I want to argue in this chapter that as servants, we must always be faithful to one priority—sharing the love of Jesus Christ with the people God puts in our lives.

Too often, Christians busy themselves with silly debates over the best way to help people experience the love of God. Some say we should show the love of Christ by our actions, being cautious not to offend others with our words. However, if we don't connect the dots between our actions and God's love, the result will be people with nothing more than fuzzy misunderstandings about God's love and grace.

On the other hand, others say we shouldn't focus on showing our love for others but on preaching Jesus to them. However, this approach often doesn't accomplish what we seek because the message doesn't line up with the actions of the messenger. Advocates of these two differing approaches are often deeply critical of each other.

Notice the either/or nature of the debate. For both sides, it is either their approach or the other approach. Might we ask, however, why is it an either/or? Or, to press the point harder, shouldn't we think of acts of service and evangelism in a both/ and way?

I firmly believe the both/and approach is the better way. Kind service and clear gospel proclamation are not antithetical to each other. Even more, they are both mandated to us by Christ Himself. So then, the doing of servanthood, which has almost limitless application, should be accompanied by clear gospel sharing. But the opposite is also true: our gospel sharing should be accompanied by clear demonstrations of servanthood. While some want to debate approaches, I want to join the two. We must serve others with our actions, and we must also share Jesus with them. Next I will highlight a few simple points about how to share Jesus as we serve.

Proclaiming and Serving Together

First Corinthians emphasizes the point I made above. In 1 Corinthians 2:1–2, Paul writes, "When I came to you, brothers and sisters, announcing the mystery of God to you, I did not come with brilliance of speech or wisdom. I decided to know nothing among you except Jesus Christ and him crucified." Paul here reminds the Corinthians of what matters most in his ministry to them. Above all else, he wants to know that they believe in Jesus who was crucified for them. For those who think all we really need to do is preach the gospel and forget about showing love through our actions, these verses may seem to make their point. After all, Paul does seem to say that preaching Jesus is what matters most. Paul wasn't concerned with impressive arguments or eloquent wisdom. Instead, he just preached Jesus.

However, this view ignores the rest of what Paul said in his two letters to the Corinthians, as well as everything He did for them when he visited them. The full picture of Paul's ministry makes clear that he cared for them in every possible way. Paul gave himself to them and served as a faithful shepherd. In 1 Corinthians 9:19–23, he describes the way he became a servant to all people for the sake of the gospel.

> Although I am free from all and not anyone's
> slave, I have made myself a slave to everyone,
> in order to win more people. To the Jews I
> became like a Jew, to win Jews; to those under
> the law, like one under the law—though I
> myself am not under the law—to win those
> under the law. To those who are without the
> law, like one without the law—though I am
> not without God's law but under the law of
> Christ—to win those without the law. To
> the weak I became weak, in order to win the
> weak. I have become all things to all people,
> so that I may by every possible means save

some. Now I do all this because of the gospel,
so that I may share in the blessings.

We shouldn't take Paul's statement in 1 Corinthians 2:2 as an indication that all we need to do is share the gospel. Such a view fails to capture Paul's full teaching and example. At the same time, Paul upholds gospel proclamation as the ultimate goal of our service to others. In Paul's teaching and example, therefore, we have both/and on display. Yes, he cared for the Corinthians and served them. He did this so that he could share the love of Jesus with them. It was not either/or for Paul, and it shouldn't be for us either.

Through kindness and service, we gain an audience with people who might not otherwise listen to the gospel. Once we have an audience, we can unpack the gospel. Jesus said, "I am the way, the truth, and the life. No one comes to the Father except through me" (John 14:6). In Acts 4:12, Peter told the Jewish leaders that there "is salvation in no one else, for there is no other name under heaven given to people by which we must be saved." Paul also wrote in Romans 5:6, 8 that "while we were still helpless, at the right time, Christ died for the ungodly. . . . But God proves his own love for us in that while we were still sinners, Christ died for us." With passages such as these, the gospel should always be on our lips around the people we serve. We demonstrate Jesus's love with our actions, but we also communicate it with the gospel.

Why Servants Proclaim the Gospel

Why should we be intentional about sharing the gospel while we serve people? As students of the Scriptures, we know that salvation cannot be achieved through our effort or spiritual labor. In Galatians 2:21, for example, Paul writes, "I do not set aside the grace of God, for if righteousness comes through the law, then Christ died for nothing."

Notice that if a person could earn merit before God through their own effort, then Christ died for no reason. Yet the Father would not have had His Son die without a purpose. Paul's point is that Jesus's death is necessary for our salvation. In Romans 4:4, Paul tells us that even if we did work for our salvation, it would count against us, not for us. Clearly, God saves not through our effort but through His saving grace found in the death of His Son. Nonetheless, most people believe that salvation is up to them. We cannot assume they understand grace; it must be made clear to them.

Furthermore, we cannot take for granted that people understand what motivates our kind service to them. While Christian love is unique and powerful, it is not uncommon for people to encounter nice people who are caring toward them. Unless we tell them about God's saving love, they may fail to understand it. Paul reminds us of the need for clear gospel communication in Romans 10. He says:

For everyone who calls on the name of the Lord will be saved.

How, then, can they call on him they have not believed in? And how can they believe without hearing about him? And how can they hear without a preacher? And how can they preach unless they are sent? As it is written: How beautiful are the feet of those who bring good news. But not all obeyed the gospel. For Isaiah says, Lord, who has believed our message? So faith comes from what is heard, and what is heard comes through the message about Christ. (vv. 13–17)

Anyone who calls on Christ will be saved. Paul assures us of this in verse 13. But Paul then asks an all-too-critical set of questions. How is it possible for them to call on Him when they haven't believed unless someone comes to them with the gospel? In short, it's impossible. Paul's point is that we have to be the conduit through which Jesus is preached to others. It is essential that we share the gospel as we serve the people God puts in our lives.

Paul concludes, "So faith comes from what is heard, and what is heard comes through the message about Christ." When we couple the gospel with our kind acts of service, we both show and speak the love of Jesus into others' lives. We cannot simply assume they understand the gospel. We have to be explicit about sharing it.

How Servants Proclaim the Gospel

Before I conclude this chapter, I should say something about our attitudes and dispositions as we share the gospel. Unfortunately, there are times when our witness becomes adversarial and abrasive. Two factors generally lead to this kind of interaction.

First, much public discourse at this moment is toxic and hostile. Our society seems to have lost the ability to have meaningful dialogue and interaction without aggression. Second, when we lack the spiritual discipline to cultivate the virtues the Bible calls us to and the example set for us by Christ, we approach dialogues with nonbelievers as a sort of rhetorical competition. We can end up treating the person we are talking to as an opponent and the dialogue as a debate. Our witness becomes hostile rather than compassionate. It is adversarial, not filled with grace. We must remember that we are called not just to share the gospel but to do so with gentleness and respect.

Several passages of Scripture provide helpful guidance. In 1 Peter 3:13–17, Peter writes to believers who have been scattered far and wide by persecution. As they sought to win people to Christ who were often hostile to them, Peter had a key message for them. Given that our world is increasingly hostile to us, we should pay careful attention to what Peter has to say in this passage.

> Who then will harm you if you are devoted to what is good? But even if you should suffer for righteousness, you are blessed. Do not fear them or be intimidated, but in your hearts regard Christ the Lord as holy, ready at any time to give a defense to anyone who asks you for a reason for the hope that is in you. Yet do this with gentleness and reverence, keeping a clear conscience, so that when you are accused, those who disparage your good conduct in Christ will be put to shame. For it is better to suffer for doing good, if that should be God's will, than for doing evil.

Peter reminds believers that suffering for Jesus's sake is an honor. He tells them to be ready to "give a defense," a phrase Christian apologists often use as a launching point for their ministry. The implication is that we should be ready to provide rational argumentation and proof for why Christianity is true.

While I certainly believe that such arguments and evidences are valuable for our witness and that it is good for some believers to be equipped for apologetics ministry, it is unlikely this is what Peter had in mind. We must remember that Peter was a blue-collar fisherman, not a philosopher. The "reason for the hope" that is in us, therefore, is likely a charge to share our testimonies of how Christ changed our lives. When people wonder why we love Him the way we do, we respond by telling them how He changed us, how He brought us hope, how He healed our broken hearts, and how He gives us joy. Therefore, we share who Christ is in the way Peter instructs us, with "gentleness and reverence."

In other words, as those who proclaim Christ to the broken people of this world, we proclaim Him with gentle spirits, showing reverence and respect to the people with whom we speak. There is no place for arrogance, sarcasm, tension, or abrasiveness in our witness. The words we speak matter, and the way we speak those words matters, too.

Another critical passage is Matthew 10:16–25. Jesus says, "I'm sending you out like sheep among wolves" (v. 16). Sheep are harmless. They don't have an attacking or abrasive disposition. Sheep don't have the ability to hurt anyone. Wolves could easily devour them.

We're reminded in this passage to be harmless, even when the people we minister to seek our harm. Jesus also instructs us to be "as shrewd as serpents and as innocent as doves" (v. 16). Given the hostility of our world, our witness calls for both wisdom and kindness. We need wisdom to navigate tense moments and hard discussions, and we need wisdom to know the time to speak and the time to remain silent. But we also need to make sure our witness is accompanied by the kindness we have found in our Lord.

Jesus further reminds us of our need to depend on Him and His Spirit. He says, "But when they hand you over, don't worry about how or what you are to speak. For you will be given what to say at that hour, because it isn't you speaking, but the Spirit of your Father is speaking through you" (Matt. 10:19–20). Notice how drastically different this instruction is from the wisdom of the world. We might think that displays of power or eloquence are most needed in sharing the gospel, but Jesus calls us to depend on the Holy Spirit and to take the disposition of harmless sheep and doves. Such an approach runs contrary to the wisdom of this world, yet witnesses who follow it are powerful in the hands of God.

Servanthood requires both acts of service and gospel proclamation. Not only are the two unopposed to each other, but they are also required of us. The either/or debate is not just silly but detrimental to our kingdom witness. We need to embrace a both/and approach that joins the two together. As followers of Jesus Christ, our servanthood can manifest itself in nearly every action of our lives, but it should be accompanied by an explanation of the love of God in Jesus Christ that alone can change lives.

Chapter 8

Servants and the Great Commission

S everal years ago I came to a simple understanding of what it means to be a follower of Jesus Christ. In virtually every sermon I now preach, I contend that we shouldn't get philosophical or abstract about it. Rather, we should view a follower of Jesus as someone who goes where He goes, does what He does, loves what He loves, affirms what He affirms, and is about what He is about. In other words, we should understand the concept of "following" literally. If we aren't doing what He did, loving what He loved, and the like, then we really aren't following Him.

This principle applies well to the concept of servanthood. A servant of Christ is someone who has given himself to Jesus's passions, loves, burdens, work, teachings, and mission. If we are not giving ourselves to these things, then we aren't serving Him.

With this understanding in mind, in this chapter I call our attention to one of the things Jesus loved, cared for, was burdened by, and gave Himself to. As the servant of the Father, He came on mission to bring redemption not just to the children of Israel but to all the people of the earth. Those of us who aspire to be His servants must give ourselves to the same mission. Serving Him means we devote ourselves to His passions, His desires, and His intentions. Jesus said this Himself: "If anyone serves me, he must follow me. Where I am, there my servant also will be" (John 12:26).

Therefore, this chapter will focus on servanthood and the Great Commission. I contend that as Jesus's servants, we must be faithful to give ourselves to His kingdom task. I'll start by reminding us that God's desire, from Genesis to Revelation, has always been for the nations. I'll then show that Christ the Son came into this world to provide salvation for people in every tribe, tongue, language, and nation. Then I will end by noting God's call on us, His servants, to take up the gospel and go to the nations. I pray that we will see God's heart for the world and that, in seeing it, we will offer ourselves in service to the same.

God's Desire for All the Nations

A common question new believers often ask is, "Why did God choose one particular group of people, the Jewish people?" "What makes them so special?" "Why does God only care about them?" The language of "a chosen people" can give the impression that God was only interested in this select group. Some of Israel's rival kingdoms thought of the God of Israel similarly, as a tribal God much like their own. In their minds, God's "jurisdiction" was over Israel only, with nothing to give and no power over anyone else. Yet this perspective has always been incorrect.

Even a partial look at what the Old Testament says about God reveals the opposite. He is not a tribal God, caring only for one group of people, with power and jurisdiction only over them. Rather, God is the God of all gods, King of all kings, and His desire has always been for all the nations, not just one.

One of the first places we see this is in God's call to Abraham in Genesis 12:1–3:

> "The LORD said to Abram: Go from your land, your relatives, and your father's house to the land that I will show you. I will make you into a great nation, I will bless you, I will make your name great, and you will be a blessing. I will bless those who bless you, I will

curse anyone who treats you with contempt,
and all the peoples on earth will be blessed
through you."

God's call to Abraham to leave his father's house and land
would undeniably be countercultural, costly, and sacrificial.
Yet God promised He would make Abraham a great nation
and protect him, cursing anyone who curses him and blessing
anyone who blesses him. What is most important for us to
notice is the statement that "all the peoples on earth will be
blessed through you."

Earlier, in Genesis 3:15, God promised through a curse
on the serpent that He would bring war to Satan and destroy
him through the birth of a child. This child would bring
redemption and victory where Satan brought destruction.
Now, in Genesis 12, God promises his assurance of victory
and redemption would come through Abraham's bloodline.
Putting it all together, we see that the child of redemption
and blessing to all people would come from Abraham's seed,
something Matthew highlights early in his Gospel (Matt.
1:1–2). God's plan has thus always been for all the peoples of
the earth, not just the Jews.

We also see God's interest in all the peoples of the earth
in the way He issues judgment in the Old Testament. For
example, notice in Exodus 9:14–16 how God speaks about
his judgment of plagues on Egypt: "For this time I am about

to send all my plagues against you, your officials, and your people. Then you will know there is no one like me on the whole earth. By now I could have stretched out my hand and struck you and your people with a plague, and you would have been obliterated from the earth. However, I have let you live for this purpose: to show you my power and to make my name known on the whole earth."

Who is the audience God has in mind? His judgment is designed not just to get the attention of Pharaoh and the Egyptians; it is designed to get the attention of all the nations. God stops short of completely obliterating the Egyptians so that "the whole earth" may see His power and His mercy. Clearly, God has more than just Israel in mind as He issues judgment on the earth. He wants not only His people but all nations and peoples of the earth to know that He is God.

In Deuteronomy 28:9–10, just before the children of Israel leave the desert and enter the Promised Land, God reminds them of the need for obedience. He urges them to obey so that He might bless them, and in that blessing, all the nations would know who He is. He said to them, "The LORD will establish you as his holy people, as he swore to you, if you obey the commands of the LORD your God and walk in his ways. Then all the peoples of the earth will see that you bear the LORD's name, and they will stand in awe of you."

God promises He will establish Israel in such a way that "all the peoples of the earth" will stand in awe. They will see the blessings the Lord gives His people. In other words, the Israelites were to be a witness and testimony of God's goodness for all to see. Just like God's judgment in Exodus 19, God's blessings to His children are meant to display His nature to all the earth.

There are dozens of other examples of God's interest in the nations. In Isaiah 5:26, for instance, the prophet writes, "He raises a signal flag for the distant nations and whistles for them from the ends of the earth. Look—how quickly and swiftly they come!" God signals for the nations and works in such a way that they see Him and are drawn to Him.

In Isaiah 42:1, God promises to "bring justice to the nations" through His Messiah. Some other examples of God's desire for the nations in the Old Testament are subtle enough that we may miss them at first glance. However, a careful look discovers them and sees their implications.

God desired the nations all along, not just a single group. He is the God of all people, not just a tribal deity with limited interest and jurisdiction. Since God's attention is on the nations, His servants' attention should be, too. The follower of Jesus will love what He loves and will want what He wants. If God wants the nations to come to Him, then so should we.

God's worldwide focus becomes even more clear as we engage prophecies of the Messiah. There we see that God not only has interest in and desire for all the nations, but He also sent His Son, the Servant Messiah, to bring redemption for people in every tribe, every tongue, every language, and every nation.

The Messiah Comes for All the Nations

The theme of Jesus's salvation for all peoples is found throughout the Old Testament and New Testament. Psalm 2, for instance, contains a dialogue between the Father and the Son. In Psalm 2:7–9, the Son speaks about His inheritance from the Father. He says, "I will declare the LORD's decree. He said to me, 'You are my Son; today I have become your Father. Ask of me, and I will make the nations your inheritance and the ends of the earth your possession. You will break them with an iron scepter; you will shatter them like pottery.'"

Here we see the Father promising that all nations of the earth will belong to the Son as His inheritance. The Son will also bring justice and peace to the nations, as He will defeat the wicked kingdoms of earth with His scepter, crushing them like broken pottery. In the end, the nations will be His, and people from each nation will worship Him.

Isaiah 42 illustrates the same point. In Isaiah 42:6–7, the Father says to the Son, "I have called you for a righteous purpose, and I will hold you by your hand. I will watch over you, and I will appoint you to be a covenant for the people and a light to the nations, in order to open blind eyes, to bring out prisoners from the dungeon, and those sitting in darkness from the prison house."

The wording in this passage is perfectly clear. The Messiah is not only for the Jewish people. He came to make a covenant for *all* people, people of every language and tongue. He came to open their eyes, allowing them to see and experience God's salvation.

In Isaiah 49, Jesus's global purpose is even clearer. Here God says, "It is not enough for you to be my servant raising up the tribes of Jacob and restoring the protected ones of Israel. I will also make you a light for the nations, to be my salvation to the ends of the earth" (v. 6). Where Israel failed in being a light of salvation to the nations, the Messiah would be successful. He would come to all people and bring salvation with Him.

The prophet Daniel echoes this promise. In his apocalyptic message about the coming kingdom, Daniel tells us how the Messiah will reign:

> "I continued watching in the night visions, and
> suddenly one like a son of man was coming

with the clouds of heaven. He approached the
Ancient of Days and was escorted before him.
He was given dominion and glory and a kingdom, so that those of every people, nation,
and language should serve him. His dominion
is an everlasting dominion that will not pass
away, and his kingdom is one that will not be
destroyed." (Dan. 7:13–14)

Daniel sees Christ coming before the Father and the
Father giving Him glory and power over all the earth. He will
not only rule over all nations; He will also be glorified by all
nations. His kingdom will be made up of people from everywhere who serve Him. His rule over them will be everlasting,
not temporal.

In Revelation 7:9, John sees a vision of those who have
been saved by the Son. "After this I looked, and there was a
vast multitude from every nation, tribe, people, and language,
which no one could number, standing before the throne and
before the Lamb." Notice how similarly the Old and New
Testaments present Jesus as the Messiah for people of every
nation. John writes that those who have been saved "cried out
in a loud voice: Salvation belongs to our God, who is seated on
the throne, and to the Lamb!" (v. 10).

Throughout the passages above and many others, Christ
the Messiah is lifted up as the Savior of all the peoples of the

earth, not just Israel. He loves them, comes for them, will bring justice to them, and will reign over them. If this is what Jesus is about, then it is what we should also be about as His servants. Servants of the Lord will care about the nations and give themselves to the task of the Great Commission.

This calling becomes crystal clear in the next section where we explore Jesus's direct call on His servants to go to the nations.

Christ Calls His Servants to Go to the Nations

A servant who follows Christ goes where He goes and does what He does. If this is true, then the servant will share the Lord's interest in seeing the nations discover the life-giving grace of our Lord. It is evident from Scripture that God has always desired the nations and that the Messiah came to bring redemption to the peoples of the nations. Christ also sends His servants directly to the nations. Consider just a few examples of His call on His followers' lives.

Starting with perhaps the most known example, Jesus instructed the disciples in Matthew 28:18–20 to take the gospel to all people. He said, "All authority has been given to me in heaven and on earth. Go, therefore, and make disciples of all nations, baptizing them in the name of the Father and of the Son and of the Holy Spirit, teaching them to observe everything I have commanded you."

Jesus came on mission to bring redemption to all the peoples of the earth, and He now calls those of us who follow Him to do the same. He envisions people from all over the world knowing Him and walking with Him as disciples, and He calls us to be a part of bringing this into existence. In places where Christ is not known and His grace is so desperately needed, His servants take the message of the cross to them. As His followers, we prepare ourselves to take the message of hope and redemption to the darkest places in the world, places where people are oppressed, brokenness is tangible, and lostness is pervasive. There in those places, as His servants, we share the wonderful hope of our Savior Jesus Christ.

John's Gospel reminds us that Jesus sends us into the darkness. Just before His death by crucifixion, Jesus prayed for His followers: "As you sent me into the world, I also have sent them into the world" (John 17:18). Three chapters later, Jesus is crucified, buried, raised from the dead, and begins to appear to His disciples. In chapter 20, He comes into a room where the disciples are gathered to send them forth. Surprising them with His presence, He says, "Peace be with you. As the Father has sent me, I also send you" (John 20:21).

In Acts 1:8, right before Christ ascended into heaven and told the disciples to wait for the Holy Spirit, He appeared to them one final time to reiterate His desire for them. He said, "You will receive power when the Holy Spirit has come on you, and you will be my witnesses in Jerusalem, in all Judea and Samaria, and to the ends of the earth." Jesus promised His disciples that the Holy Spirit would be with them and would empower them in their service to Him. He also made clear that He would use them to be His witnesses both near and far, "in Jerusalem, in all Judea and Samaria, and to the ends of the earth." Those of us who serve Him today must recognize that He seeks to use us to bring salvation and redemption to the nations as well.

Before we conclude, I want to look at one more passage that might be overlooked if we aren't careful. In Romans 1:14–16, Paul teaches us that the gospel is for all people and that we have an obligation to take it to them. He says, "I am obligated both to Greeks and barbarians, both to the wise and the foolish. So I am eager to preach the gospel to you also who are in Rome. For I am not ashamed of the gospel, because it is the power of God for salvation to everyone who believes, first to the Jew, and also to the Greek."

Paul's language is startling. He speaks of our role as one of obligation. Given what Christ has done for us and that He seeks people from every tribe and tongue, we now have a responsibility to take up. We now share in the task of getting the gospel to people all over the world.

I've tried to demonstrate in this chapter three general themes about God and the nations found throughout the Scriptures: (1) God has always desired the nations, not just the Jewish people; (2) the Messiah came to bring redemption to all the nations, not just the Jewish people; and (3) Jesus Christ calls His disciples to take the gospel to every nation, every tribe, every tongue, and every language. But why have I included all this in a book about servanthood?

The application for us is simple. If we are following Jesus, then just as He cares for the nations, we will too. If we aspire to be His servants, then we will serve Him in seeking the nations with Him. We cannot be His servants if we ignore the nations or our hearts are cold or indifferent toward them. He loves the nations, and His servants will, too. As we seek to serve Him, one of the most central things we do is give ourselves to the Great Commission.

For some of us, this may mean that we move our families overseas and serve in a full-time capacity as missionaries. For others it may mean that we go on short-term trips, give financially from what God has provided for us to those who go in our place, or pray faithfully for those doing the work. Each of our roles will differ. But as those who are following Him and serving Him, we must be a part of this work. That is because followers go where He goes, do what He does, and are about what He is about.

Chapter 9

Philippians 2– Servanthood in the Life of Jesus Christ

Throughout this book we have turned our attention to the most important aspects of servanthood. In this final chapter, I want to consider the passage from which the book—*Let This Mind Be in You*—derives its name. In Philippians 2:5, Paul gives us a command that is essential to this book's message, but even more essential for our lives: "Adopt the same attitude as that of Christ Jesus."

The full chapter of Philippians 2 provides one of the most beautiful portraits of our Lord Jesus, as the apostle Paul describes for us what He was like and how He lived. Just as Christ humbled Himself as a servant, we are called to do the same. Before we look more closely at the chapter, though, I'd like to remind us of the problems I set forth in chapters 1 and 2. In response to these problems, I point to Philippians 2.

In chapter 1, I noted the selfish dispositions that bring untold brokenness into the world. In chapter 2, I considered the way many of us can become prideful and arrogant in ministry. Instead of being fountains of humility and grace the world so desperately longs to see and know, we can become much like the world.

I don't mean to dismiss the wonderful aspects of many believers and their ministries. God has done so many good things through so many over the years, wonderful things we must retain and preserve as we move forward. In the worst version of ourselves, though, we become the opposite of what we are called to be. When we're not mindful of our own sin and pride, we put ourselves on a dangerous path. The next thing you know, we have made idols out of our own names and live to serve those idols. Like a peacock, we become people who puff up and strut around.

I remember as a young boy going to the zoo on a field trip. We looked at the elephants, the giraffes, and all kinds of different animals. But I distinctly remember the peacock. The zookeeper talked about how small the bird is compared to how big it appears once it stretches out its feathers. With feathers out, peacocks prance around, show off, and pretend to be much bigger than they actually are.

I remember the zookeeper mentioning how beautiful the peacock is. I have to admit, however, I thought the peacock was foolish. Unfortunately, a peacock is the best analogy for what we, the very ministers called to be humble servants, are like when pride and arrogance take control in our hearts. In the worst version of ourselves, we are peacocks. We puff out our feathers, strut around, and pretend that we're bigger than we actually are. None of this is what we are called to be or to do in Christ. One way to understand the command given to us in Philippians 2 is to think about what Paul would say to the peacock inside us. His instruction would be clear: "Kill the peacock!"

As profound as Philippians 2 is theologically, I believe the great Christological portion of it is offered to us primarily as an illustration of the servanthood we are called to. Having charged us to "do nothing out of selfish ambition or conceit" and to "look not to [our] own interests, but rather to the interests of others," Paul now tells us to "adopt the same attitude as that of Christ Jesus." Just as the divine Son took on the posture of a servant, we are called to do the same. Consider carefully Paul's words in 2:1–11.

> If, then, there is any encouragement in Christ,
> if any consolation of love, if any fellowship
> with the Spirit, if any affection and mercy,
> make my joy complete by thinking the same

way, having the same love, united in spirit, intent on one purpose. Do nothing out of selfish ambition or conceit, but in humility consider others as more important than yourselves. Everyone should look not to his own interests, but rather to the interests of others.

Adopt the same attitude as that of Christ Jesus,

> who, existing in the form of God,
> did not consider equality with God
> as something to be exploited.
> Instead he emptied himself
> by assuming the form of a servant,
> taking on the likeness of humanity.
> And when he had come as a man,
> he humbled himself by becoming
>   obedient
> to the point of death—
> even to death on a cross.
> For this reason God highly exalted him
> and gave him the name
> that is above every name,
> so that at the name of Jesus
> every knee will bow—

in heaven and on earth
and under the earth—
and every tongue will confess
that Jesus Christ is Lord,
to the glory of God the Father.

A Call for Unity and Selflessness

I want to highlight three important aspects of this passage. Notice first the call to unity and selflessness in Philippians 2:1–4. Paul instructs us to unite together for the cause of Christ and to be selfless in so doing. In other words, we're called to be people who think more about one another and the cause of Jesus than we do about our own names, our own brands, our own reputations, and our own platforms. We are called to die to ourselves for others and the cause of Christ.

In verse 2, Paul writes, "Make my joy complete by thinking the same way, having the same love, united in spirit, intent on one purpose." What does he mean? He is suggesting that the people of God ought to have a unity about them that is different from what is found in the rest of our world.

If you pay attention to anything happening in our world right now, it's easy to see the dysfunction, brokenness, and divisiveness that rage. Our world divides on every possible front, along racial lines, political lines, athletic lines, musical lines, and so many more. It ought to break our hearts that it's often not much different among the people of God. We, too, can divide on almost every conceivable point.

Yet if ever there were a people on earth who ought to be able to rise above divisiveness, it should be people who have been healed by Christ from their brokenness. It should be people who have tasted the sweetness of Christ, people who have been redeemed by His great mercies. This is exactly who Paul calls us to be in verse 2. One of the essential ways we are supposed to be different from the world is in our unity achieved through Christ.

What are we supposed to be united about? What's involved? Does unity mean we somehow manage to get along? Probably not. It doesn't merely involve playing nice with one another even though we are different. Notice the way Paul describes our unity. He writes, "Make my joy complete by *thinking the same way, having the same love*" (emphasis added).

We need to go back to Philippians 1 to understand what he's referring to. In 1:16–18, Paul notes that some "preach out of love, knowing that I am appointed for the defense of the gospel; the others proclaim Christ out of selfish ambition, not sincerely, thinking that they will cause me trouble in my imprisonment. What does it matter? Only that in every way, whether from false motives or true, Christ is proclaimed, and in this I rejoice. Yes, and I will continue to rejoice." In other words, what matters most to Paul and what can allow unity to form within the body of Christ is a shared burden to ensure that the gospel is preached to those who need to hear it.

Look also at Philippians 1:21. In verses 19–26, the apostle Paul wonders whether it's better for Him to die and go to be with Jesus or to remain in the flesh and continue laboring as a servant, discipling others so that they may be made strong in Jesus. His response to this question is in 1:21, where he writes, "For me, to live is Christ and to die is gain."

What is he saying throughout chapter 1? He's saying all that really matters among us is Christ and His kingdom. This outlook is the context for 2:2, where he writes, "Make my joy complete by thinking the same way, having the same love, united in spirit, intent on one purpose." He is telling us that our love for Jesus and His kingdom ought to be enough to unite us in Christ.

The call for unity is not all we see, though. Paul goes on to remind us to be humble toward one another. In Philippians 2:3–4 he says, "Do nothing out of selfish ambition or conceit, but in humility consider others as more important than yourselves. Everyone should look not to his own interests, but rather to the interests of others." This is the central command in the chapter for us to consider.

We are to be like Jesus in regard to humility and servanthood. We're commanded to be a people who, like Jesus, look out for the interests of other people more than we look out for our own interests. The peacock won't let us do that, will he? The peacock likes to spread out his feathers, strut around, and show everybody just how big, how beautiful, and how important he is. Where we are naturally inclined to look out for and make much of ourselves, we are called to follow Christ in humility, caring for other people first.

The Example of Jesus Christ

The second aspect of this passage I want to highlight is the example of Jesus Christ that Paul gives us. In Philippians 2:5, Paul writes, "Adopt the same attitude as that of Christ Jesus." He's instructed us in Philippians 2:3–4 to be selfless servants; now He shows us what servanthood looks like. He does so by expounding upon Jesus's condescension from glory to earth.

"Adopt the same attitude as that of Christ Jesus." Pause right there. What does this mean? It means that you and I are to adopt Jesus's mindset in the way we approach life, other people, and our ministries. You and I are to adopt the posture of His heart and the disposition of His mind. What was His mindset? Paul writes that Christ, who existed "in the form of God, did not consider equality with God as something to be exploited. Instead he emptied himself by assuming the form of a servant, taking on the likeness of humanity. And when he had come as a man, he humbled himself by becoming obedient to the point of death—even to death on a cross" (Phil. 2:6–8).

Although Jesus possessed a divine nature and all rights to glory and honor, He humbled Himself to serve us. We're commanded to adopt that same mindset and live within it. His disposition was one of humility, obedience, sacrifice, trust, and devotion. It was not one of an arrogant peacock who makes much of itself.

An important theological discussion normally arises from this passage. Specifically, scholars often refer to 2:6–11 as the great kenosis passage in the New Testament—*kenosis* meaning "Jesus's emptying of Himself." What does *kenosis* mean? It doesn't mean that He emptied Himself of His deity. It means that as the divine Son entitled to all the glory, honor, and power, He lowered Himself by coming as a man, becoming a servant, and giving His life over to death, even the harsh death of the cross. We are called to emulate His humility.

Philippians 2 is also one of the four great Christological passages from which we get our richest theology of Christ, the other three being John 1; Colossians 1 and 2; and Hebrews 1. This passage teaches us that Jesus is the divine Son, possessing the divine nature, who came in the likeness of humanity, possessing real human nature. One can and should legitimately glean such insights from the text, but Paul's primary purpose was not to make a theological point. His primary reason for writing these words about Christ was to give us an example of what Christian servanthood is supposed to look like.

"Adopt the same attitude as that of Christ Jesus" is Paul's way of telling us to adopt Jesus's posture of heart and mind. Like Him we are supposed to be servants. Even though He is God, He "emptied himself by assuming the form of a servant." To follow Jesus's lead, we have to kill the peacock. As Christ followers, we go where He goes, do what He does, and live as He lived. Jesus was no peacock, so we shouldn't be either. He humbled Himself as a servant, so we should, too.

It's amazing how much more we could do for God's kingdom if we didn't care about our own reputations, brands, and platforms. In Christ, God Himself, the one who spoke and brought the universe into existence, took the form of a humble human being. Not only did He come in the form of a man, but He also humbled Himself and became obedient to the point of death, even death on a cross.

Clearly Christ wasn't concerned with His brand or platforms. He was concerned with the kingdom of God and with our redemption. For this I am thankful because in Him we have salvation and life. Just as the Father used Christ to bring redemption to us, what might He do with us if we likewise followed Christ's example of humility and servanthood? Friends, as Paul urges us, let's "adopt the same attitude as that of Christ Jesus."

Jesus modeled servanthood again in John 13. The disciples came into the room after walking dirty streets. It was hot, and they were sweaty and filthy, especially from about the knee down. The foot washer was the lowest job anyone could have, and typically a slave would take up the towel and the basin to wash people's feet. Yet our Lord Jesus, the one who brought everything into existence with a simple word, took a towel and a basin, stooped, and washed the filth from His disciples' feet.

Afterward, Jesus said to the disciples, "If I, your Lord and Teacher, have washed your feet, you also ought to wash one another's feet" (John 13:14). His point was simple, and it is the same as Paul's point in Philippians 2. Christ is our example, and we are supposed to follow Him.

Christ Our Reward and Joy

The command in Philippians 2 is substantial. We are called to humble ourselves and become servants. We can't help but wonder in response, "What's in it for me?" This is the wrong question, but even so, we inevitably ask it. A paradigm shift has to transpire in our minds.

We tend to think obedience to Jesus and our happiness run in opposite directions, such that we must choose between them. If that were true, following Christ in humility would be a difficult choice. But please hear me. As Paul reminds us in Philippians 2, obedience to Jesus is not about losing our joy. Rather, obedience to Jesus is about living and finding fulfillment in the one who made us, who has infinite wisdom, and who loves us perfectly. Our pursuit of Him is always for His glory and our good. To find Him is to find life itself.

Jesus said, "A thief comes only to steal and kill and destroy. I have come so that they may have life and have it in abundance" (John 10:10). Admittedly, obedience to Jesus includes moments where we must let go of something we love or want. In letting go, though, we find that what we thought would be bitter actually becomes sweet and life-giving. What's in obedience for you? In a word: life. But it is life that only Christ can give.

Paul points all of this out to us in Philippians 2. He reminds us that our experience with Christ motivates us to give our lives as servants. In verse 1 he writes, "If, then, there is any encouragement in Christ, if any consolation of love, if any fellowship with the Spirit, if any affection and mercy." In other words, Paul wants you to remember what you encountered in Jesus. He wants you to remember what you were like when Christ found you.

Do you remember how broken you were? Do you remember the shame and guilt that saturated the depths of your being? Can you also remember the sweetness of meeting Christ in those first moments? Can you remember how He began to pick up the broken pieces and put you back together?

Is there is any encouragement in Christ? Yes! Is there any consolation in His love? Yes! Is there is any fellowship in His spirit? Yes! Is there any affection and mercy in Him? Yes! My friend, if you've tasted and seen that the Lord is good (Ps. 34:8), then "adopt the same attitude as that of Christ Jesus." If you have known the great satisfaction that comes from knowing Christ, then kill the peacock and be His servant!

A Prayerful Reflection on Servanthood

As we conclude the book, I want to circle back to some of the main themes we've considered together. More specifically, I want to encourage self-reflection in light of what we found.

We considered the brokenness of our world and how greed, pride, and self-centeredness bring harm and pain into our lives. In response, we must examine ourselves to see where such appetites control our thoughts and actions. When I do so, I sense the Lord's conviction for my tendency to care more for myself than for others. Each of us must ask the hard questions about where greed, pride, and self-centeredness show up in our lives and how we intend to respond to them. I pray that for me and you both, we won't simply read chapter 1 and walk away from it without examining our hearts.

In chapter 2, we looked at the desire in each of us to be affirmed; the unique mix of experiences in ministry that cause us to crave attention, spotlights, platforms, and applause; and the lack of spiritual discipline to deal with these sinful cravings. These three factors create a perfect storm, causing those called to humility and servanthood to become egocentric, prideful, and selfish. No one intends for such traits to develop, but they do. It happens far more frequently than we'd like to admit.

I pray that each of us can see ourselves clearly and not read chapter 2 without pausing to reflect on the ways that we, too, are prone to seek platforms and applause or to worship the idol of our own names. Spotlight and applause are not what our lives should be about. Seeking them doesn't please the Lord, and it certainly doesn't satisfy our souls. As we reflect on chapter 2, I pray that we will become more intentional to seek the Lord's forgiveness, to humble ourselves before Him and others, and to aspire to the servanthood to which we are called.

In chapter 3, we saw that great biblical figures were themselves servants. They were people of great humility, obedience, sacrifice, trust, and devotion. More importantly, in chapter 4, we observed that Jesus Christ, as He is presented to us in both the Old Testament prophesies of Isaiah's Servant Songs and in the New Testament, was the ultimate servant of the Lord. He embodied humility, obedience, sacrifice, trust, and devotion in the fullest sense, and in doing so, He modeled for us what our lives should look like.

I pray that as we look at Him, we will long to know Him more deeply and to become more like Him. In writing this chapter more so than any other, my sense of conviction grew with every page. As I considered Him, I became convicted over how dissimilar I am to Him, yet I was also inspired by Him. As we see the beauty of the Son, I pray that our hearts will be stirred to the point of transformation. Pray that the Lord will cultivate in you a disposition toward humility, obedience, sacrifice, trust, and devotion.

In chapter 6, we discovered that servanthood is the only possible way for us to give our lives. Since the servant must give it all, it is necessary that he first find it all. Only when we learn to find our true delight in Christ will we be freed from the idolatrous charms of this world that keep us from full surrender. But when we come to see His worth, His goodness, and His beauty, the world begins to grow dim and faint.

I pray that we will see Him. I pray that we will learn to delight in Him. I pray that we will come to know the beauty and satisfaction of God that the psalmist knew in Psalm 63, that Paul knew in Philippians 3, and that Jesus spoke of in Matthew 13. In knowing Him, I pray that you and I will love

Him more than anything else in this world and give ourselves to be His servants. Together, may we seek Him, find Him, and give our all for Him.

In chapters 7 and 8, we considered our responsibilities as servants to share the gospel with broken people, both here and among the nations. We can't separate the words we preach in the gospel from our actions, and our actions should be the acts of a servant. Gospel sharing and service are not either/or but both/and. When we give ourselves to both, there is great power that can only come from God.

Additionally, as His servants who are devoted to following Him, we must go where He goes. As the servant of the Lord came to bring salvation to every tribe, every tongue, and every people, we should be concerned with the same. I've sometimes heard believers say, "God hasn't put the nations on my heart." It may be true that God has not called you to live your life overseas, but as a follower of Jesus, the nations should always be in our hearts. Missions is one of the central ways we follow and serve Him.

Therefore, I pray that concern for the nations will stir our hearts. I pray that we will go ourselves, send our sons and daughters, support our brothers and sisters as they go, and pray regularly that God will do a great work among the nations through us. He came as the Savior of the nations. I pray that we will leverage our lives for this mission.

I close with a simple word of challenge. I suspect that many of the folks who have read this book may be Southern Baptists. If so, as a fellow Southern Baptist, I praise God for you, my brothers and sisters. In the best version of ourselves, we are servants. But in the worst version of ourselves, we have created a massive ecosystem to be lords and masters over. In our systems and institutions, we can strive for the high seats and positions of honor.

God has no interest in your kingdom or mine. He is building the kingdom of His Son, and His "kingdom is an everlasting kingdom; [His] rule is for all generations" (Ps. 145:13). I don't want to live another moment of my life investing in anything except God's kingdom, and I pray that you don't either.

For everyone who reads this book, the only way to invest in God's kingdom is to follow Christ, who, though He is God, "did not consider equality with God as something to be exploited. Instead, he emptied himself by assuming the form of a servant, taking on the likeness of humanity. And when he had come as a man, he humbled himself by becoming obedient to the point of death—even to death on a cross" (Phil. 2:6–8). Echoing Paul, I charge myself and you to "let this mind be in you also" (v. 5 NKJV).

Scripture Index